THE
DAILY
Check-In

THE
DAILY
Check-In

A 60-DAY JOURNEY
TO FINDING YOUR STRENGTH,
FAITH, AND WHOLENESS

MICHELLE WILLIAMS

NELSON
BOOKS

An Imprint of Thomas Nelson

PREFACE

*H*ey there, my beautiful, brave, courageous, and fearless readers. I'm so glad you're here.

First, I want to say how proud I am of you. Picking up this journal is a step. It's a step in the direction of wholeness and healing. And you deserve wholeness and healing. You deserve to live a full life—a life without the crippling anxiety and shame so many of us are lugging around.

I don't know where you are in your journey. Maybe you're going through something terrible. Heartbreak. The loss of a loved one. Depression. Or maybe you just feel stuck. You're caught in a holding pattern and don't know how to break the cycle. Or maybe your mama told you to read this, so you're reading it. *That* I get. What Mama says, goes. Mind your mamas, y'all!

Wherever you are in life, I want you to know that this is a safe place. When you're writing down your thoughts, they don't have to be perfect. For some of my fellow perfectionists, this is gonna be tough! But try and let go. Respond from the heart—even if your thoughts are scattered. Ask God to open your mind, to bring back memories you may have forgotten or suppressed. If you want to come back later and make sense of your answers, do it. But you don't have to.

This journal is an invitation to *freedom*. And sometimes the road to freedom is messy. Okay, *most* of the time the road to freedom is messy. If you need to cry, let the tears flow, sis. If you feel angry, lonely, sad, let yourself experience those emotions. They're legitimate, and they're valid. You don't have to hide here.

I am praying over each and every word you write. But more than that, God is watching. He's listening, and he cares. He's with you. You are not alone.

Blessings,

Michelle

CHECKING IN

Before we get too far, I think it would be helpful to explain or remind you what it means to check in.

In my experience, there are three ways I can check in that make my life and being myself better, easier, and far more peaceful.

1. **Check in with God.** I'm not talking about on-the-go, knee-jerk prayers—though there's nothing wrong with those. I'm talking about carving out consistent, gut-level time with God. Because until we start talking to him regularly in an honest, sometimes R-rated way, our check-ins with God will be on the surface. When we can look at ourselves and say, "God, I acknowledge we've got a hot mess over here, but I know you can help fix it," then we will see life change and freedom.

2. **Check in with you.** Sometimes this is the hardest habit to get into. We're busy, we're tired, and when we get a minute alone, we want to check *out*, not in. But this step matters because we can't be honest with anybody until we've been honest with ourselves. We have to get

in the habit of looking in the mirror and asking tough questions. Heck, take yourself on a date! Put it on the family calendar. And we've got to be kind to ourselves.

3. **Check in with others.** This one has become so incredibly important to me. If it weren't for the people I have in my life, I literally don't know what would have happened to me during my darkest moments. This one is also the most difficult for me. I'm a private person. I don't like to share my business with folks. But what I've learned is that when you cultivate relationships with the right people—people who love God and love you—you'll be dragging them into your business every chance you get. And you'll *all* be better for it.

Out of the three ways we can check in, which do you find the *easiest*?

_____

_____

_____

_____

_____

Which is the biggest challenge to you?

_____

_____

_____

_____

_____

What do you hope to gain, change, or experience through checking in?

_____

_____

_____

_____

_____

_____

_____

What will be the biggest obstacle in achieving those things?

_____

_____

_____

_____

_____

_____

_____

Can we agree on something right now? Can we agree that we're in this thing together? Can we promise each other that we won't give up on learning how to check in, even if it feels hard, impossible, even indicting at times?

I'm walking this road with you, sis. I'm beside you. I'm for you. And together, with God, there ain't nothing we can't do.

HOW TO USE
THE JOURNAL

This journal will be most effective when it's used side by side with my book, *Checking In*.

Each journal entry is divided into five parts: read, think, hear, respond, and pray.

In the read section, you'll find portions of text from my book that introduce an idea or theme that we'll dig into a little deeper together throughout the rest of the entry.

In the think section, we'll talk about different ways that an idea or theme may play into your life—how it may hurt you or help you when it comes to checking in.

In the hear section, we'll dive into the Word of God together to see what he says about the topic.

In the respond section, I'll ask you to process and reflect on our learning. The goal of this section is to help you personalize the content and find practical ways to apply the teaching to your daily life.

Finally, in the pray section, I give you a starting point

to connect with God, lifting up everything you're working through, processing, and learning about checking in.

My prayer is that checking in with God, yourself, and others will be not only a tool in your spiritual toolbox but also a lifestyle of vulnerability, self-awareness, and honesty. A lifestyle where you consistently unburden yourself of the weight of your anxiety, depression, and fears. A lifestyle of overwhelming joy, deep-rooted peace, and grace without end.

DAY 1

Read

In July 2018 I was swimming in a sea of darkness. I didn't have an exact plan for how I'd end my life, but those thoughts were quickly forming.

I'd been talking publicly about my struggle with mental illness for more than a decade, but nobody knew how bad it had really gotten. I had stopped checking in, so I was preparing to check out.

Somehow—only God can explain how—I picked up the phone. Then I said the strongest three words a person can say: "I need help."

And that's the short version of how I ended up checking into a mental health facility under a false name with my lip hair grown out to my chin and smelling like I hadn't showered in days (because I hadn't).

I checked myself into a hospital because I wasn't checking in anywhere else.

Think

Not everybody who fails to check in finds themselves in a mental health facility. In fact, most of us don't. But the fact that we're not checking in with regularity—or checking in at all—is still a major problem.

We all have our reasons. Some of them are actually pretty good. We're too busy to check in with any type of intentionality. We have families, jobs, houses to maintain, responsibilities, commitments.

Yes, all those things take up hours of our days. But let me ask you this: What might happen (or what has already happened) if we don't carve out the time to connect with our Father, ourselves, and one another?

I found myself checking off to-dos on my funeral-planning list. Maybe you're there. Maybe you're not, but life just feels heavy. Your back hurts from carrying around the weight of your own shame, anxiety, depression, hurt, and disappointment.

Sis, I pray today that you would stop trudging through life. That you would unload some of that junk you've piled up over the years. Things you can't let go of, forgive, or even acknowledge.

But you know what? Starting this journal is a step toward a lighter load. It's a step toward a lifestyle of checking in. And I am so dang proud of you. Don't stop here. Keep moving forward. You can do it—and you're not alone.

Hear

Come to me, all you who are tired and are carrying heavy loads. I will give you rest.

—MATTHEW 11:28

Respond

In recent years, what have been some of the reasons you've had for not checking in with God, yourself, and others?

_____

_____

_____

_____

Colossians 3:2 says, "Think about things that are in heaven. Don't think about things that are only on earth." How has thinking about things that are only on earth distracted you from thinking about things that are in heaven (or living out your faith)?

_____

_____

_____

_____

Pray

Father, I want everything that you promise to those who follow you. I want peace, I want joy, I want fullness of life. Help me to reach toward the light during moments of darkness. Even if they're longer than a moment. Help me to remember that you desire to connect with me regardless of my circumstances. You've made a way for me to feel hopeful when there's no other reason to hope. Thank you for your patience with me. In Jesus' name, amen.

DAY 2

Read

Like most of you, not all my experiences checking into a hotel have been amazing.

I'm not a diva, despite the full-hair-and-makeup Michelle Williams you're used to seeing on stage or TV, but my OCD cleaning at hotels is real. To this day I take my Clorox wipes to any place I check into, and I wipe down all the surfaces. And if I'm checking into somewhere for more than a few nights, I'll swing by the store and pick up some Scrubbing Bubbles, some Lysol, and a sponge too. That's when I'll really get to work.

Recently, I stayed in a luxury hotel in Los Angeles for a couple of weeks, and the shower had this beautiful gray slate tile flooring. I got out my sponge and cleaner, and by the time I was done, that gray tile was beige.

Here's my point: it takes a certain amount of personal effort to create a check-in experience that's good for our hearts. Can't nobody else know exactly what we need to say, do, or scrub to create a peaceful place for us to rest.

Think

If we want checking in to last more than a season, we've got to make it part of our lifestyle. And if we want something to become a part of our lifestyle, we've got to create daily habits that can be repeated and recreated over time.

Like I said in day 1, we're busy folks. We've got things to do. And when we're done doing the things we have to do, we're tired.

That emotional gas gauge is on E. The last thing we feel like doing is praying meaningfully, doing a self-inventory, or calling a friend to vulnerably check in.

So, how do we do it? How do we figure out how to check in consistently over time? And to do so with such intentionality that it becomes a part of our DNA? Something we do without even realizing it?

It takes practice, planning, and patience. But it can only be done by you. Because only *you* know how *you* best check in.

Hear

When you pray, go into your room. Close the door and pray to your Father, who can't be seen. Your Father will reward you, because he sees what you do secretly.

—MATTHEW 6:6

Respond

Read the following descriptions of ways people best connect to God.

1. **Nature**—This type feels most connected to God when they're outdoors enjoying his creation. Taking a hike, watching the sunrise, or standing in awe of a beautiful mountainscape reminds them of how big and great our God is.

2. **Tradition**—This type feels most connected to God when they're engaged in a traditional practice of their faith. Maybe that's going to church, taking Communion, or fasting—they're reminded of a faithful God through ancient spiritual practices.

3. **Art**—This type feels most connected to God through artistic expression. Painting, drawing, writing, even listening to music draws them closer to the God of all creation.

4. **Care**—This type feels most connected to God through acts of service. Caring for others, giving generously, or volunteering to serve reminds them that Jesus is a king *and* a servant.

5. **Justice**—This type feels most connected to God when they're able to defend those who can't defend themselves. Advocating reminds them that God's love is offered to all his people—regardless of age, gender, socioeconomic status, or race.

6. **Studying**—This type feels most connected to God through intellectual stimulation. Listening to sermons or theological podcasts and reading the Bible reminds them of the vast, complex nature of God.

Out of the six above, which do you most recognize in yourself? _____

Now that you've become more aware of how you best connect with God, how can you apply that knowledge to improve your check-ins with him?

_____

_____

_____

_____

Pray

God, your Word is clear: there are ways to check in with you that matter more than others—that help me more than others. Help me to become more aware of how I best connect with you. I desire a real relationship with you. One that is honest and vulnerable. It's up to me to create the best environment for that to happen. Give me wisdom in how best to check in with you. I love you. In Jesus' name, amen.

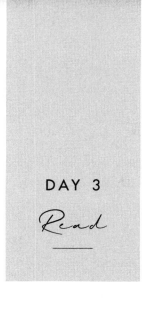

DAY 3

Read

Things don't always go our way. Bad things do happen. And if we're not owning the responsibility to check in the right way, the bad things can make us forget all the awesome things God has done for us already.

I can so clearly see the fingerprint of God on the map of my journey, and it makes me wonder how I could ever fall into seasons of disconnection and doubt in my faith.

But I do. We all do. That's because a relationship with God is just that—a relationship. It needs the same care, attention, and communication as any other growing, changing relationship.

Yes, we do live in a fallen world where people hurt themselves and one another on a daily basis. But we *can* check in with ourselves when that happens and remember all that God has already done for us.

Think

We've all been there before. We're going through life, minding our own business, when disaster rains down on us like a surprise summer storm. Maybe we saw the clouds rolling in, or maybe it came as a complete shock. Either way, life suddenly became complicated. Hard. Maybe it even felt unmanageable.

I've been there. More than once. It ain't fun, and it sure ain't pretty.

We've got to remember one simple, resounding fact: the goodness of God is not based on the circumstances in our lives. The goodness of God is based on the cross. And nothing, nothing that happens during our time on earth can contradict his display of selfless, furious, and relentless love and compassion for you. I am telling you, honeeeeyyyy! That's a truth worth checking in with.

Hear

I have told you these things, so that you can have peace because of me. In this world you will have trouble. But be encouraged! I have won the battle over the world.

—JOHN 16:33

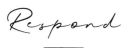

Respond

What are the times in your life when, looking back, you can clearly see the fingerprint of God on your story?

_____

_____

_____

_____

What is your typical reaction to the "trouble" we're promised (conflict, change, loss, rejection, failure, etc.)?

_____

_____

_____

_____

If your first reaction to life's challenges isn't to check in with the truth of who God is, what he's already done for you, and who he says *you* are, what is one thing you can do *this week* to make that shift?

_____

_____

_____

_____

_____

Pray

God, I want to create a lifestyle of checking in. I want to be emotionally and spiritually prepared whenever life showers me with adversity. I want to react to trials and struggles by checking in with the truth of who you are and remembering all that you've already done for me, which is far and above what I deserve. I love you, Father. Amen.

DAY 4

Read

As a society, we value certain bags, jeans, and luggage sets not because there's anything unique about them, but because of the *who* behind the *what*. We define designer items by the designer.

If we define a bag based on its creator, why don't we define ourselves by the same standard?

Let's think about the one who created us, God. The process of how we were dreamed up and planned for and loved on and created by God surpasses our ability to understand.

So when we fail to see the beauty, the perfection, the completeness of his creation—us—what are we communicating to God? What are we communicating *about* God? Basically, we're saying we know better and can do more than God can.

Because we're defined by our Maker, we need to pay attention to *how* we're defining who we are.

Think

Have you ever spent a little (or a lot!) extra on something because of its label? No shame here, friend. Your girl is guilty of it too!

Now, let me ask you this. If you do or did own a designer bag, how would you treat it? Would you leave it out in the rain? Kick it around? Call it ugly, stupid, or useless? Nope. I bet you wouldn't. I bet you'd treat that bag like the queen it is.

Imagine this. You're out shopping with some girlfriends and you see something in a store that grabs your attention. You think, *I'ma need that.* So, you walk inside and flip the tag to see whose creation it is—and just cannot believe what you've found.

It's a God original.

Literally—sent from heaven to the showroom floor. There isn't another one like it in existence.

Okay, tell me right now you wouldn't freak out. Because I sure would. Something dreamed up, planned out, and created by the very mind and hands of our heavenly Father?

Add. To. Cart!

Why do you think it's so hard for us to view ourselves the same way we'd view this imaginary purchase? Why is it so hard for us to grasp that we are purposeful, brilliant, and extraordinary masterpieces created by a God who longs to be in relationship with us?

Until we can begin to see ourselves this way, the way God sees us, we will struggle to check in with him *and* with ourselves.

Hear

How you made me is amazing and wonderful.
I praise you for that.
What you have done is wonderful.
I know that very well.
None of my bones was hidden from you
when you made me inside my
mother's body.
That place was as dark as the deepest
parts of the earth.
When you were putting me together there,
your eyes saw my body even before it was
formed.

—PSALM 139:14–15

Respond

What negative thoughts do you find yourself thinking about yourself on a regular basis? Take your time and really consider what your mind tells you when you look in the mirror. Or when something disappointing happens. Or when you mess up. Write those thoughts down. Anything you think about yourself over and over again.

For me, it's always been, *I don't bring anything to the table. I'm not valuable. I'll always be seen as a background accessory.*

What are those recurring negative thoughts for you?

_____

_____

_____

_____

_____

_____

_____

Now, go back to our Scripture reading for today. Read it again. Underline any part of that verse that contradicts the things you tell yourself. Whose words are you going to let define you—yours, society's, or God's?

Pray
___

Father, we live in a society that is constantly reminding us of what we lack. Everywhere we turn, we see someone who appears to have more and be more. But that is not how you want me to live. You want me to see myself the way you see me—as a God original. As a one-of-a-kind masterpiece. Believing this is critical in helping me check in. Remind me of this truth anytime I begin to doubt my worth. In Jesus' name, amen.

DAY 5

Read

Back when Destiny's Child was at its height, we'd do the craziest things to keep our identities under wraps while traveling, especially when checking into hotels. I'd come up with the most ridiculous fake names to check in with: Barney Rubble. Rudy Huxtable.

We all want to protect our identities in certain scenarios, right? And yet we accept labels that define our identities without even questioning them.

- *I'm still single. That must mean I'm going to be single forever.*
- *I haven't had a baby. That must mean I'm never going to be a mother.*
- *My man left. That must mean I'm not worth loving.*

All those labels—I had allowed them and even embraced them. Because I wasn't testing my thoughts. I wasn't challenging my own words. I wasn't checking in with myself.

The only label I've got that matters is *God's. God's creation. God's work. God's child.*

Think

Have you ever had someone use your identity without your knowledge? Someone steal your credit card information, birthday, Social Security number, or name?

If you have, I bet you got pretty fired up about it. If you haven't, I'm sure you can imagine the outrage you'd feel over it. How *dare* someone mess with what's yours—your identity—who you are and what you've worked for?

Yet we hand over our identities every day to people who don't even know us.

Someone made a comment or a judgment, and we *owned* their words like they were from God himself. We traded what God says about us for what they said about us.

Why? Why are we so quick to personify the bad and so slow to embrace the good? I think it's due to a lack of checking in. Most of us aren't even aware of how we think, feel, and talk about ourselves.

Hear

See what amazing love the Father has given us! Because of it, we are called children of God. And that's what we really are!

—1 JOHN 3:1

Respond

Who am I right now?

_____

_____

_____

_____

_____

Who do others say I am?

_____

_____

_____

_____

_____

Who do I say I am?

_____

_____

_____

_____

_____

_____

Now crack open that Bible (or Bible app) for a hot minute. Read through the scriptures below (or choose a few and read those). Then answer the final question.

- I say I am unlovable, but God says I am forever loved (Romans 8:38–39).
- I say I am damaged, but God says I am healed (Isaiah 53:5).
- I say I am weak, but God says he makes me strong (Psalm 18:32).
- I say I am a failure, but God says I am forgiven (1 John 2:12).
- I say I don't belong, but God says I am adopted into his family (Ephesians 1:5).
- I say I am broken, but God says he makes me whole (Colossians 2:10).
- I say I have been rejected, but God says I am his (Isaiah 43:1).
- I say I am alone, but God says he is always with me (Joshua 1:9).
- I say I am hopeless, but God says I can have hope (Jeremiah 29:11).
- I say I am purposeless, but God says I was created with purpose (Esther 4:14).
- I say I have failed, but God says I am victorious in Jesus (1 Corinthians 15:57).
- I say I am lost, but God says he gives me direction (Isaiah 30:21).
- I say I am worried, anxious, or afraid, but God says with him I can find peace (John 14:27).

- I say I am unhappy, but God says I can be joyful no matter what (John 15:11).
- I say my head is a mess, but God says I am powerful, loved, and have a sound mind (2 Timothy 1:7).

What are two or three of the labels above that you need to embrace most right now?

_____

_____

_____

_____

_____

_____

_____

_____

Pray

Father, I have based my identity on labels others have given me for far too long. I am ready to check in with myself—I've got to if I want to live the full, joy-filled life you offer me. I'm ready to do this regularly so I can diligently monitor my thoughts and feelings toward myself. I want only your labels to define me. I love you, Lord. Amen.

DAY 6

Read

Have you ever had someone do you dirty? (We all nod yes because, duh.)

I had a guy friend working for me whom I was very close with. Let's call him Nathan. Nathan and I were basically family. He was thorough, sharp, and thoughtful. Then one day, I got an email from Nathan. Only, this email didn't come from his regular work email address; it came from *another* work email address. Like: YourLyingEmployee@YourCompetitor.com.

Well that can't be right, I thought. *He works for me.*

Nathan's actions reinforced some of my most crippling insecurities at that time—that I was just a stepping-stone to the next, better thing. When I found out what he'd done, I blew my lid. Nathan's actions were wrong, but how I reacted sure wasn't right.

Without checking in, I had become completely unaware of myself.

Think

Are you a stuffer or an exploder? I think we can be both. The more we stuff, the bigger the inevitable explosion.

But when we're stuffing, it's like we don't even know it's happening.

Have you ever gotten up from a good meal only to find yourself moving slower than molasses? You're beyond full. You're overflowing. You're downright miserable.

It's easier than you think to stuff yourself to the point of discomfort without even knowing it.

During the situation with Nathan, I remember knowing that I was a little more freaked out than the circumstances called for. Problem was, I was no longer in control of my reactions. I couldn't calm down. I couldn't get ahold of my thoughts, emotions, or myself.

I had exploded.

And if you would have asked me how I was doing at that time, my surface answer would have been, "Fine. Okay. Just doing life over here." You know? But the truth is, I wasn't taking the time to evaluate anything on an authentically deep level. I wasn't checking in.

Hear

God, see what is in my heart.
Know what is there.
Test me.
Know what I'm thinking.

—PSALM 139:23

Respond

Which of the following describes you best? Put a check beside all that apply:

- I often find myself feeling overwhelmed without knowing why.
- Sometimes the smallest thing can set me off.
- My anger does not always make sense in light of the offense I'm angry about.
- Sometimes I walk around feeling like a ticking time bomb of emotions.
- The people closest to me have said they feel like they have to "walk on eggshells" around me.
- Sometimes I feel intense emotions without knowing why.

If any of these are true for you, there's a good chance you're not checking in with yourself or your emotions regularly.

Now write out three things that you *want* to be true about you—about your emotions, character, and reaction to adversity.

1. _____

2. _____

3. _____

How can checking in with yourself help make the things you just listed true?

_____

_____

_____

_____

_____

Pray
___

Father, help me to remember how important it is to guard my heart. God, I want to be vigilant. I want to be someone who is aware of my thoughts and feelings. Help me to test my thoughts by checking in with myself and with you on a regular basis. Amen.

DAY 7

Read

I remember the first time I realized there was something off with my emotions. I was a junior in high school. I knew that I was kinda sad all the time, but I couldn't tell you the first reason why. I was isolating myself, losing interest in things I used to love, and my grades started dropping.

Classic symptoms of depression. But I didn't have a name for it. I didn't feel like I looked like a person who would be considered depressed, you know? But of course, I've learned that depression does not always have a look.

Then, in my twenties, while I was still in Destiny's Child, I remember telling someone on our team at the time, "Hey, I feel like I might be depressed." And he was like, "What do you have to be depressed about? You guys just signed a multimillion-dollar deal. You're about to go on tour. You guys are about to release your own Barbie dolls."

By the time I got my actual diagnosis of clinical depression, I was thirty years old.

Sometimes, when we check in, we realize things about

ourselves that we don't like. But no matter what we find, we can't give up. God is still God, regardless of what we find when we start checking in.

Think

Have you ever played with a toddler? One of my favorite things toddlers do is hide their faces and think that just because they can't see me, I can't see them. It's funny, y'all.

We laugh at kids, but we have a similar mindset when it comes to checking in. We hesitate to check in because we're afraid of what we'll find. And if we do check in, and we get the slightest glimpse of something we don't like, we either immediately assign blame to others or just give up and quit.

If I don't dig too deep, then whatever I thought I saw doesn't exist.

Just like a toddler.

But if I'd stopped checking in after I realized I had real, clinical depression, I don't know where I'd be today. In fact, I might not be at all.

Hear

Take a good look at yourselves to see if you are really believers.
Test yourselves. Don't you realize that Christ Jesus is in you?

—2 CORINTHIANS 13:5

Respond

Underline any of the following statements that sound similar to something you've told yourself recently:

· I'm good. I'm fine. I just need to move on.
· The past needs to stay right where it is—in the past.
· It is what it is.
· I wouldn't be this way if it weren't
  for _____.
· There's nothing I can do to change who I am.
· I shouldn't feel this way. I should feel grateful.
· I don't have time to figure out these feelings. It's exhausting.

If you underlined any one of those, think about this: Does avoiding reality make reality any less real?

What, if anything, are you afraid you'll find if you check in with yourself vulnerably and consistently?

_____

_____

_____

_____

_____

_____

_____

_____

When I realized I needed help with checking in, I knew I needed the guidance of a professional therapist to deal with what I found.

If you find something you don't like or want to change while checking in, what are a couple of healthy ways you can deal with it?

_____

_____

_____

_____

_____

_____

_____

_____

Pray

God, if I can have the courage to check in with myself in a real way, there's a good chance I'm going to see some things I don't like. Some things I'm not proud of. But I know that this is part of a process that you want for me. Give me wisdom, Lord. Show me how to confront the ugly side of checking in—because I know that will lead me closer to who you want me to be. In Jesus' name, amen.

DAY 8

Read

We've all felt at least a little depressed before, right? Maybe your experience is a little different from mine. Maybe you started feeling depressed after a specific event. Maybe *depressed* isn't even the term you would use, but you started feeling disconnected from things and people, including yourself.

You lost a job. Your man left. Your child was born with a diagnosis. A loved one passed away. Someone you looked up to disappointed you. God didn't answer your prayers the way you thought he would.

At some point, you stopped asking yourself the hard questions:

- Have I been letting myself feel my feelings?
- Am I withholding forgiveness from myself or others?
- What lies am I believing to be the truth?

You stopped checking in—like I had.

Think

Depression. What response do you have to that word?

- Shame—because Christians aren't allowed to be depressed?
- Anger—because someone you needed used their depression as a reason to desert you?
- Pain—because no matter what you try, you can't shake the feelings of despair that haunt you?

I grew up thinking that if the Holy Spirit lived in me, then I should never feel lonely, scared, or depressed. But that's not what the Bible teaches. It says, "God gave us his Spirit. And the Spirit doesn't make us weak and fearful. Instead, the Spirit gives us power and love. He helps us control ourselves" (2 Timothy 1:7).

We are guaranteed dark seasons in life. But when we experience those, the Bible says that *through God's Holy Spirit* we can lean the weight of our hard feelings on him.

Hear

God gave us his Spirit. And the Spirit doesn't make us weak and fearful. Instead, the Spirit gives us power and love. He helps us control ourselves.

—2 TIMOTHY 1:7

Respond

If you're not leaning the weight of your hard feelings on God, you're leaning them on something or someone else.

Which of the following things, people, or habits do you tend to lean into when you're experiencing disappointment, depression, or anxiety:

- Food/sugar
- Exercise
- Shopping
- Alcohol
- Cigarettes
- Your spouse
- Your friends
- Medication
- Sleep
- Isolation
- Social media/internet

Add any of your other coping mechanisms that aren't listed above.

_____

_____

_____

_____

_____

Some of these things are healthy. Some aren't. But if you aren't turning first to God in the difficult seasons of life, other coping mechanisms are not going to be effective.

What would it look like for you to lean the weight of your hard feelings first on God's Holy Spirit?

_____

_____

_____

_____

_____

_____

_____

_____

_____

_____

Pray
___

Father, thank you that you've given me a way to feel strong when I am weak. Through the power of your Holy Spirit, I don't have to walk through dark times alone. In the moments when I don't feel like I can carry on, remind me that you want to carry me through. Amen.

DAY 9

Read

Looking back, I see my childhood as a time when I learned to cover up what was really going on. Checking in of any sort was not encouraged. We swept everything under the rug and went about our lives as if everything and everyone was happy. I never learned how to talk about what I was feeling because no one around me did.

Maybe you can relate. Maybe it's hard for you to check in with yourself because you're not even sure what that looks like. Or maybe your parents were the opposite and overshared. Maybe they couldn't stop talking about themselves, what they were feeling, and what they'd been through or were going through. Maybe you've gone the other direction in your own life because they were just too much.

Think

Studies show that many of us have a black-and-white reaction to the way we were raised.[1] We either identify with parts of our parents' personalities and become very like them, or we run the complete opposite direction to become *nothing* like our parents.

One problem with both of these reactions is that neither is authentically us. We're becoming who we are based on who others were.

After years of therapy I realized that, in many ways, I had embraced both types of reactions to my childhood. There were pieces of my personality that weren't really me. And just like basing our identities on others' labels, it's unhealthy to base our identities on the actions of others.

Part of checking in with yourself is asking, *Do I have any habits, beliefs, or traits that aren't authentically mine?*

Hear

I have thought about the way I live.
And I have decided to follow your covenant
laws.
—PSALM 119:59

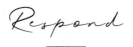

Respond

For each statement below, mark if it is true of your relationship with any of your parents by writing "M" for mother, "F" for father, "SM" for stepmother, and "SF" for stepfather. If it's untrue of any of your parents, write nothing.

_____ I was rarely or never told, "I love you."

_____ I was treated as though I was too sensitive, too emotional, or too needy.

_____ I was made to feel like my emotions weren't valid.

_____ We never talked openly about faith.

_____ My parent was often angry at others.

_____ We kept secrets from each other.

_____ When we had a conflict, my parent did not work to repair my hurt and resolve the issue.

_____ If I got angry, I was punished or rejected.

_____ Even as I got older, I was not trusted to make my own decisions.

_____ We didn't talk openly about personal challenges, failures, or hurts.

Which of your responses has held you back *most* when it comes to checking in?

_____

_____

_____

_____

Pray

God, help me to take a close look at my life so that I can see when I'm not being authentically *me*—the person you created me to be. We all have childhood wounds, no matter how wonderful our parents were. Help me to check in when I am reacting out of those wounds so I can bring them to you. Amen.

DAY 10

Read

Early on in counseling, my therapist would say, "How does that make you feel?" all the time. And my answer would always be the same: *Mad. Pissed off. Angry. Frustrated.*

But she was patient. "Think back to what happened. What thoughts did you have right before you got mad?"

That was harder to answer. Take the Nathan situation, for example.

"What were you thinking?"

I was thinking he's an idiot. I was thinking he's a traitor. I was thinking he is dead to me.

"Before that. What were you thinking?"

That he used me. That he didn't see me as valuable. That I was worthless, just a means to an end.

Whoa. That whole time, I'd been walking around with my anger, thinking I had a right to be mad. When really, I was just feeling like no one would ever see me as valuable for *me.*

Because I wasn't being honest with myself and checking in, I had no idea that feelings of worthlessness were at the root of my anger.

Think

If you have the same reaction to most of life's challenges, it's probably time to check in with the thoughts you have about yourself.

Think back to the last time someone hurt or wounded you. What was your reaction? What internalized beliefs and thoughts may have caused that reaction?

For example, if your knee-jerk response to difficulty is

- *hopelessness*, maybe you need to check in with your faith;
- *apathy*, maybe you need to check in with your priorities; or
- *rage*, maybe you need to check in with some unforgiveness you're hanging on to.

Our reactions mirror our thought processes and belief systems. What do yours say about you?

Hear

A person might think their own ways are right.
But the LORD knows what they are thinking.
—PROVERBS 21:2

Respond

Think about the last time you responded inappropriately to something or someone.

What were the thoughts behind the emotion?

_____

_____

_____

_____

_____

_____

_____

In hindsight, how would you have handled that situation differently?

_____

_____

_____

_____

_____

_____

_____

Pray

Father, help me to be a person who checks in with the thoughts I'm having before I have an emotional reaction. You know my mind and heart better than I do. Show me how to pinpoint false belief systems, bad logic, or worn-out faith. I love you. Amen.

DAY 11

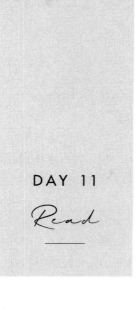

Read

In 2005, in the same bomb-dropping fashion that I had landed my gig with Destiny's Child, it ended.

The disappointment that followed threatened to pull me under like a riptide.

Have you ever had that happen to you? You had this master plan laid out, and all of a sudden somebody came along (life came along) and lit a match at all four corners?

Maybe you got married, but he left.

Maybe you've had your baby names picked out since middle school, but you can't conceive.

Maybe you've worked your butt off to hit that goal, but it always seems to move just out of reach.

We've all experienced this. Life goes left when we thought it was going right, and we catch a sucker punch that sends us reeling. And if we're not checking in the way we should be, it can quickly erode the stable ground beneath our feet.

Think

Preparing for the unexpected sounds impossible, right? Because it's just that—unexpected. But what if I were to tell you that there's a way to make the unexpected not quite so jarring?

That's one of the most powerful benefits of checking in— it's a practice that stabilizes you. Because it centers your life on the unchanging love and promises of God.

Think about it this way. You're riding in a car, and all of a sudden somebody crashes into you. Talk about unexpected. If you're wearing your seat belt, you may walk away with some cuts and bruises. If you're not wearing a seat belt, you may not walk away at all.

Checking in with God is the best seat belt we have against life's unexpected crashes. You buckled up for what is promised to be a bumpy ride?

Hear

You are my rock and my fort.
Lead me and guide me for the honor of
your name.
—PSALM 31:3

Respond

What is a "crash" you have experienced in life that you didn't expect?

_____

_____

_____

_____

If you could ask God one question about that situation, what would it be?

_____

_____

_____

_____

I want you to do something for me. It's gonna feel a little weird, but just give it a try: ask God that question. And sit for a few minutes in silence and see what you hear. What you feel. Write down anything you sense in your spirit.

_____

_____

_____

_____

_____

Pray

God, help me to prepare my heart for life's crashes—both big and small—by relying on you and your Holy Spirit to anchor me. Remind me to check in with you, my best source of comfort and refuge, when the unexpected happens. You are my rock. You are my fortress. You guide me. Amen.

DAY 12

Read

After Destiny's Child ended, I decided to put out an album called *Unexpected*.

I knew that the world would be watching how it did, and the pressure felt like I was walking around with a big ole gorilla hanging from my back. But still, I was excited. And in fall 2008, my first-ever dance album dropped.

And dropped.

And dropped—down the charts.

Unexpected didn't do as well as I or anyone had hoped. And my music career was put on ice. Ice in the back of one of those walk-in freezers in the industry's basement.

When I looked around, it felt like everybody was succeeding—everybody but me.

But if I had checked in with all that was *good* in my life, I would have seen that I had so much to be grateful about.

Think

Have you ever been let down by an outcome?

I mean, I might as well ask if you've ever walked the face of the earth because if you've been alive for longer than fifteen minutes, chances are, something or someone has disappointed you.

You know what *loves* disappointment? Depression. In fact, left unattended, disappointment is a breeding ground for depression. And the more we feed our disappointment by comparing our lives to the lives of others, the more likely we are to stay stuck in a state of depression.

Any math fans reading? If not, no worries. I'll keep it simple. Here is a little equation that shows my experience with disappointment:

Disappointment + Comparison = Depression

Comparison is like pouring gasoline on the spark of depression. And if you're not checking in with your thoughts, your whole house can catch on fire before you even smell the smoke.

Hear

Am I now trying to get people to think well of me? Or do I want God to think well of me? Am I trying to please people? If I were, I would not be serving Christ.

—GALATIANS 1:10

Respond

Can you think of any people from the Bible who struggled with failure or disappointment? How did they handle it? (If you can't think of any, choose from the list below and read their story before answering.)

- Adam and Eve (Genesis 3)
- Naomi (Ruth 1)
- Noah and his sons (Genesis 9)
- Sarah (Genesis 16)
- Aaron and Miriam (Numbers 12)
- Moses (Numbers 20)
- Samuel and his sons (1 Samuel 8)

_____

_____

_____

_____

The last time you felt deeply disappointed, what role did comparison play in making the situation better or worse?

_____

_____

_____

_____

_____

Now write a short gratitude list. What do you have to be thankful for today?

_____

_____

_____

_____

_____

_____

_____

_____

_____

_____

_____

Pray

God, remind me to check in with my feelings of disappointment. Help me to remember that you're with me always, not just when things are going well. Convict me of comparing myself to others. I know that the story you are writing with my life is unique, so help me to remember your faithfulness in times when it feels like I'm the only one failing. Amen.

DAY 13

Read

A relationship with God is just like a relationship with anyone else. Sometimes you feel really close to each other and sometimes you don't. It all depends on how much time you've been spending together and how much effort you've been investing into the relationship.

For a lot of people, there is something really appealing about being close to God. But I know that's not the case for everybody. Maybe the idea of being close to God sounds great, but it's also kind of intimidating.

Maybe you're afraid to feel close to God. Because if you were to get honest with God and check in with God, you might hear him say something you don't want to hear.

Think

Think about the course of your relationship with God. In the times you've been most closed off from God, it's likely that this distance came out of anger, guilt, or fear.

Almost any time I've been distant from God, I've struggled with a little bit of all three. Maybe I was afraid to hear something like, "Now that I've got you where I want you, let me get out my list of all the ways you've screwed up lately" or "Let me tell you all the reasons I'm mad at you."

For many of us, God reminds us of an angry parent or grandparent who always finds something wrong with us. So, we keep our distance. But can I tell you something? I know exactly zero people who have said, "I started checking in with God, and everything in my life went downhill from there."

Whatever your reasons are for not checking in, they sure don't compare to the benefits you'll get from an honest, open, close relationship with the Father.

Hear

The LORD is ready to help all those who call out
   to him.
He helps those who really mean it when
   they call out to him.
—PSALM 145:18

Respond

I want you to list all the things, people, thoughts, and feelings that are keeping you from being as close to God as you want to be.

_____

_____

_____

_____

What can you do today to remove some of those obstacles and grow in your relationship with our Father?

_____

_____

_____

_____

Pray

Father, forgive me for any way I have failed to trust in your good and compassionate character. Remind me when I am fearful that you want what's best for me. Show me how to face my fear of checking in with you so that I can stay close to you. Amen.

Read

Have y'all ever heard of a guy named Abraham? He was a pretty big deal in the Bible.

God showed up and spoke to him in some sort of vision or dream. He told him to leave the country he was living in.

If it's me, I'm like, "God, I've got questions. You want me to do what? Leave my family and friends? For how long? What am I supposed to tell my mama? And wait a minute—you want me to go where? I need details, Lord! A timeline. And a map, if possible."

God asked Abraham to take a big step. But there was a promise attached. He wasn't asking Abraham to leave his life so that he would be miserable, but so that he would have a life that he had never imagined. Basically, God wanted more for Abraham. But Abraham had to take the first step in faith, with no timelines and no guarantees of what this "better" future would look like.

Think

Are you a person with a plan? You got that to-do list written out every morning and an itinerary printed off before every vacation? Ain't no shame in being a planner. Planners make the world go round!

But what would you do if checking in with God led you to take a step into the unknown?

What would you do if God told you to give up something or someone you didn't want to give up? Go somewhere you didn't want to go? Stay somewhere you didn't want to stay?

It's all fun and games until checking in messes with our plans.

But just like with Abraham, if God asks something of you, it comes with a promise—that he is working all things together for your good (Romans 8:28). That he will not leave you or forsake you. That he has the best plan of all—his perfect will for your life.

All you have to do is take that first step in faith.

Hear

I will make you into a great nation.
And I will bless you.
I will make your name great.
You will be a blessing to others.
I will bless those who bless you.
I will put a curse on anyone who puts a
curse on you.
All nations on earth
will be blessed because of you.

—GENESIS 12:2–3

Respond

What are things or plans that you are holding on to and not giving over to God? List them out and then release them to God.

_____

_____

_____

_____

_____

Pray

Father, sometimes checking in with you will cause a change of plans. And that can be scary. That's hard. God, help me to remember that when you ask something of me, it's always attached with a promise of your faithfulness to walk with me every step of the way. Amen.

DAY 15

Read

You want to know something cool about God? He's always there.

No, really. Think about it.

He doesn't take vacations to Cabo and leave somebody else in charge. He doesn't nap or get on Twitter. God always stays exactly where he is.

So, when I feel far from God, I can be sure of one thing: it's a *me* problem, not a God one.

After Destiny's Child broke up, I was depressed. I allowed that depression (and disappointment) to come between me and God. For a brief time, my disappointment became bigger than my faith. And I stopped checking in with him.

As a result, my entire world felt off-kilter. I was in a constant state of anxiety and moodiness.

Think

We've already said that our relationship with God is just like our relationship with anyone else—it requires an investment of time and energy on our part. But how do we reconnect with him in a real, honest way? Especially when we're still hurt and angry?

For me, that's where I started—with my hurt and anger. I told God I was pissed. That's right. I said those exact words. And you know what? God was okay with it.

Now, change didn't happen right away. But the more I prayed real, honest prayers, the more I was releasing my control over my life and future. And I felt more at ease. More at *peace*. I felt God's presence, even when things around me weren't necessarily changing in a way I could measure.

Change may not always happen when we want it to or how we want it to. But you can be sure of this—when we check in with God, it *does* change things. It moves us closer to our Father.

Hear

Send me your light and your faithful care.
Let them lead me.
Let them bring me back to your holy mountain,
to the place where you live.

—PSALM 43:3

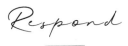

Respond

If you were to pray a gut-level, nonfiltered prayer to God right now, what would you say? Write it out.

_____

_____

_____

_____

_____

_____

Now I want you to do something bold. I want you to pray that prayer. Do it! God can take it. Also, just to let ya in on a little secret, he already knows everything you're thinking and feeling anyway. Talk to him. Read what you wrote word for word and check in with God authentically right now.

Pray

God, you've heard my gut-level words, and you know my deepest feelings. Please help me through this season and help me to grow closer to you in the process. In Jesus' name, amen.

DAY 16

Read

I don't know what this says about my taste in men, but my first crush growing up was the organ player at my church.

I was about five years old. He was dating my older cousin who used to babysit me. Years later, they're happily married with kids. He's actually still a phenomenal musician and an all-around awesome guy.

And that was probably the last all-around awesome guy I had a crush on.

Y'all, I'm kidding. I really am. I've dated plenty of great men in my day, but I've also dated some men that make me look back and think, *Michelle, you are smarter than that. You knew better than that, girl.*

Nope. Not crazy. Just so critically out of touch with myself that I thought it was normal to allow a man to date me without ever admitting publicly that he was dating me.

One of the most common side effects of not checking in is not knowing what you want, need, or deserve. And suffering because of it.

Think

You know what I hate? Laundry. It doesn't matter how often I do it—it seems like more and more dirty clothes creep into those baskets. Like they're in there mating or something.

Just the other day I was looking for this specific sports bra. I couldn't find it. Not in my drawers. Not in my closet. Then I remembered—shoved in the back of my guest room were clothes hampers. Filled with dirty laundry. I went through two of them before finding the dang thing.

As I was shoveling through the mounds of nasty clothes, I found at least ten other things I'd been looking for. Things shoved down because I didn't feel like dealing with them.

In that moment, I was reminded of my life before I started checking in.

I would stuff everything down. Everything that felt hard or uncomfortable. Everything that led to any type of resistance. Everything including the things I wanted or needed out of a relationship. I became a punching bag. An easy target. A victim.

Not checking in made me stupid, y'all. And God don't make stupid.

Hear

An honest answer
is like a kiss on the lips.

—PROVERBS 24:26

Respond

Think through your closest relationships—whether they're romantic or relationships with friends, family members, or colleagues. Are you checking in (being honest) with yourself about your wants and needs in those relationships?

If you're not being honest in these relationships, what are you shoving down? What would you say to those people if you were being honest?

NAME   **WHAT YOU NEED TO SAY**

_____   _____

_____   _____

_____   _____

_____   _____

_____   _____

Pray

God, you created us as people who have needs, wants, and dreams. You wouldn't give those to us if you wanted us to shove them down and ignore them. You don't want us to be doormats or to allow ourselves to be treated as less than. Help me to be brave enough to check in with myself and live by my convictions. I love you. Amen.

DAY 17

Read

I saw a quote from Hart Ramsey on Twitter that hit me hard: "If you don't heal properly after leaving a dysfunctional relationship you will end up in a different version of the same relationship you just escaped from."[2]

I've heard quotes or sayings like this before, and I've nodded my head like, *Yeah, that's right. If you dysfunctional folks don't get it together, you're going to ruin it for the rest of us.*

It never occurred to me that I might be the one bringing the dysfunction. But honey, when you're the common denominator in all the drama, chances are you are the source of that drama.

If your relationships with coworkers, friends, or significant others always end the same way, that's not bad luck. That's just bad character.

Think

You ever walk by a mirror and see something about yourself that shocks you? And not in a "dang, I look kinda good today" way. More like a "there's more poppy seed in my teeth than in my stomach" kind of way.

When we take a hard look at ourselves, sometimes we see things we don't want to see. And this is especially true when looking back at our past "hurts" from relationships.

If we were honest with ourselves—I mean, like, magnified-mirror honest—we'd see traces of our own missteps, mishandlings, and mishaps in the stories we rehearse about our wounds. The truth is, there are very few conflicts in life that are 100 percent someone else's fault.

Acknowledging and owning our shortcomings is a painfully necessary part of checking in. Because then, and only then, can we seek forgiveness, change, and grow.

Hear

God is faithful and fair. If we confess our sins, he will forgive our sins. He will forgive every wrong thing we have done. He will make us pure.

—1 JOHN 1:9

Respond

Think about the last three relationship breakdowns, blowups, or conflicts you've had.

Write down what *their* part was.

_____

_____

_____

_____

_____

_____

_____

Now write down your part. You may have to spend a few minutes thinking, but if you check in vulnerably, you'll be able to name something. What could you have done differently, better, or not at all?

_____

_____

_____

_____

_____

_____

_____

Pray

God, I confess to you that there have been times I have not owned my part in the dysfunction of a relationship. Maybe I wasn't checking in with my part of the blame. I repent, knowing that you have forgiven me. If there's someone else I need to ask for forgiveness, please give me the courage to do so quickly. I love you. Amen.

When I think back to my earliest dysfunctional relationships, I have to start at home. My mom and dad's marriage, like most marriages, was far from perfect. Don't get me wrong. They worked hard. They took us to church and taught us to do right. And they stayed together.

But there were times I wish they hadn't.

We never discussed those times. That was just our family's way—image over honesty.

So when I reflect, I have to start with the relationships I have with my mom and dad. I have to ask myself some tough questions.

Ultimately, checking in led me to realize that I didn't have bad parents. I had human parents. And instead of looking to God to get my unmet needs satisfied, I have looked to romantic relationships to do that.

Think

We've established that we've all experienced childhood wounds, right? Even if we had the most loving, kind, fun parents in the world. There are ways our childhoods, in general, have left voids in our hearts and in our lives.

As humans, our first reaction is to repair those wounds by our own means. We do this subconsciously, without even realizing it.

Maybe you're a workaholic because you never experienced financial stability as a child.

Or you enter relationships with men who need fixing because that's what was modeled to you as a child. Or you don't make time for yourself because that's how your mama did things.

Many of us try to fill our own voids. But often this can lead us to further injury.

Maybe you've already checked in with the voids in your life. Or maybe, like most people, you're vaguely aware of them but don't know how to repair them to ensure they're not repeated.

I've got good news. Jesus offers us wholeness and healing through the power of his Holy Spirit. But first we have to identify those voids by checking in.

Hear

"But I will make you healthy again.
I will heal your wounds," announces the
LORD.

—JEREMIAH 30:17

Respond

If you were to look back at your first dysfunctional relationship, what would you see? Who would be there? What words would you be hearing?

_____

_____

_____

_____

What ways have you tried to repair the wounds caused by that dysfunction? What have you used to fill that void?

_____

_____

_____

_____

Are you willing to replace those void fillers with the only thing, only *one* that can actually make you whole? What would that look like?

_____

_____

_____

_____

_____

_____

_____

_____

Pray
___

God, your Word promises that you can make me healthy again. It promises that you can heal my wounds. And Father, you know that so many of us are walking around with unhealed places in our stories that desperately need to be restored and repaired. We've tried to fill those voids, but you are the only one with the power to truly bring wholeness. I ask you now to begin that process. Help me to identify and bring my unmet needs to you and only you. I love you, Father. Amen.

DAY 19

Read

I met Chad in June 2017. By July we were a couple. I trusted him. He was faithful, committed, vulnerable, and transparent.

But then the doubt started creeping in. The old patterns. Pretty soon I was consumed. I let my thoughts pick me up and carry me through the next few months.

I started constructing reasons why Chad was eventually going to abandon me. It began as an, *I'm so lucky to be his*, and quickly devolved into, *Am I a good enough Christian to be his mate? Why did he choose me?*

My thoughts got downright crazy because I wasn't checking in with myself, God, good people—no one.

Think

Have you ever relapsed?

I'm not talking about a drug or alcohol relapse (although,

those count too). I'm talking about any time you've learned a new way of thinking, living, eating, or exercising, and then, out of nowhere, you found yourself right back where you started. In old ways of thinking and acting.

You relapsed.

That's what happened not too long after I met Chad. I had been to therapy, knew I had clinical depression, and had begun the checking-in process. And honey, I was flying high. Then I crashed.

My thoughts got the better of me.

Have your thoughts ever won? In the tug-of-war of what we think and feel and what we've learned to be true, have your thoughts ever pulled you over that line of logical thinking?

That's why consistency is *key* to checking in. We can't stop—not even when we're on the pink cloud of new love. (Or a new job, new friendship, new anything!)

We can't stop checking in.

Hear

Therefore, my dear brothers and sisters, stand firm. Let nothing move you. Always give yourselves fully to the work of the Lord, because you know that your labor in the Lord is not in vain.
—1 CORINTHIANS 15:58 NIV

Respond

Has there ever been a time or area in your life where you've relapsed?

_____

_____

_____

_____

_____

_____

_____

_____

_____

_____

If checking in consistently is key to avoiding a relapse, you're going to have to be intentional. Write out your general weekly schedule. The big things. Work, kids, carpool, typical errands. What are times during at least five of those days that you can commit to checking in with God, yourself, and others? Go back and add those times into your schedule.

Stick to them—don't relapse. If you do, that's okay. We're humans. But get right back to the practice of checking in as soon as you realize you're slipping. You and God have this!

Pray

God, your Word tells me to stand firm. That's exactly what checking in consistently will require of me—a lifelong commitment to being steady and unmovable in pursuing mental, emotional, and spiritual health. And God, I may fail. I may relapse. But you're always there. Thank you for always welcoming me back with open arms anytime I want to check in with you. Amen.

DAY 20

Read

Things between Chad and me became incredibly strained.

Now, I'm pretty sure the entire world knows what happened next (spoiler alert: huge public breakdown). Since then, I've gone to the depths of hell psychologically and learned that I needed to get more real with myself and God than I had before.

I started praying. *God, show me what I'm not seeing in myself. Help me accept your unconditional love and acceptance.*

I started thinking about who I am. That being in a relationship was like offering people a muddy cup of water with twigs and tiny little bugs and dirty rocks in it, filled with the wounds I'd encountered over the years. I'd been offering that cup to everyone I loved and expecting them to look at it as if it were a crystal goblet of the finest wine.

I wondered how my life would be different if instead of my hurts and disappointments, I offered others a glass full of joy. I wondered what would happen if instead of walking around with a posture of *prove it*, I walked around with a posture of *peace*.

Think

I went hiking with a friend once. Now, I'm pretty steady at the gym. I may not be winning any Olympic medals, but your girl is active.

We got to this plateau and I stopped, looking out over the edge. It was beautiful. And I was tired.

"That was great," I said. "Should we head back down, now?"

My friend looked at me like I was speaking Greek.

"Um, this isn't the end of the trail," she told me. "We're only halfway up."

Have you ever felt this way in your own life? Like you've grown. Like you've learned. Like you've reached some pinnacle or pause in an area of your life. Only to feel a tap on the shoulder, saying, "You've got to keep going. We're not even halfway there."

That's where I was in my relationship with God. I hadn't done all the internal work that needed to be done yet, and my external relationships were paying the price.

When we're checking in like God wants us to, with who God wants us to, we offer the people we love a glass of joy. It's cool. It's clean. And it goes down easy—smooth, and refreshing.

Hear

May the God who gives hope fill you with great joy. May you have perfect peace as you trust in him. May the power of the Holy Spirit fill you with hope.

—ROMANS 15:13

Respond

Let's get artsy for a minute. Go ahead and draw what's in your mental, emotional, and spiritual "cup." Label anything you see inside it.

I'll go first. I'll tell you what my cup looked like during most of my relationship with my ex-fiancé. My cup had a twig labeled *Unforgiveness*. A chunk of mud at the bottom labeled *Unmet childhood needs*. A bug in the middle labeled *Wounds from previous relationships*. A leaf floating around labeled *Career disappointments*. That's what was in my cup, and I was ready to throw it out.

Now draw your cup.

What would it take to pick out all that yuck in your cup? What do you need to do to offer others a cup of joy instead?

_____

_____

_____

_____

_____

_____

_____

_____

_____

_____

Pray

God of hope, like your Word says, I pray that I am filled with great joy, peace, and trust in you. I know the only way to replace my muddy cup with a cool, refreshing glass of water—one free from wounds, hurts, and unmet needs—is to bring the cup I'm holding right now to you. And to keep bringing it to you over and over again, without fail. Amen.

DAY 21

Read

I know some people roll their eyes when they're asked about their childhood wounds. But maybe you're repeating what you haven't repaired. I think in some ways, we all are. And you may think, *Michelle, there's too much broken about my past to fix it.* I get what it feels like to be overwhelmed. Just choose one situation with one person. Ask yourself the hard questions:

- *Why was I so sad or angry?*
- *What thoughts were behind the emotions?*
- *What beliefs were behind those thoughts?*

I had to revisit some painful moments. I had to deconstruct some beliefs in order to construct new ones. I had to dump out my tall glass of pain so I could take my cup to God and ask him to clean it and fill it up until it overflowed in confidence of his promises.

Think

If you've been to counseling or therapy for any amount of time, there's a decent chance you've revisited your childhood wounds. Maybe your parents divorced when you were really little, so you don't believe marriage lasts. Maybe an uncle or a family friend took advantage of you, so you have a hard time trusting people, especially men. Maybe you got picked on at the playground, so you're a defensive person in general.

If you're living your life today from a wounded place, it's very possible you are living your life, at least in part, at whatever age you were when the hurt took place.

- How much of the three-year-old you is living your life right now?
- How much of the seven-year-old you is living your life right now?
- How much of the twelve-year-old you is living your life right now?

I want you to know that that person *matters*. And that person is *important*. But that person is no longer you. You can move forward. You can accept, forgive, and let go (finally!). Because your past self doesn't need you—but your present and future self desperately do.

Hear

Forget the things that happened in the past.
>Do not keep on thinking about them.
I am about to do something new.
>It is beginning to happen even now.
>Don't you see it coming?
I am going to make a way for you to go through
the desert.
>I will make streams of water in the dry and
empty land.

—ISAIAH 43:18–19

Respond

Look back on your life. List any hurts or wounds that you can recall from each age group. If you can't think of any, that's fine. List one that comes to mind from the following ages:

0–5: _____

5–10: _____

10–15: _____

15–18: _____

Now circle one or two of those wounds that you suspect may still be affecting your life today.

If you could go back to that version of yourself and say something to her, what would you say?

_____

_____

_____

_____

_____

_____

Can you tell that girl to move on? Can you tell her it's time to let go?

Pray
___

Father, thank you so much for the gift of another day. For the opportunity to sit down and check in with you. God, I have been hurt. We all have. I have *caused* hurt. We all have! But I don't want to bring the past into my present. I want to give up all hope of having had a better past. Please help me release the grip I have on any past wounds, be fully present in the now, and know that you have something better for me in the future. Amen.

DAY 22

Read

Are you the type of person who carefully reads anything you're agreeing to? Like cell phone agreements, insurance coverage agreements—anytime you click that green I Agree button—do you read the tiny text first?

I don't. Ain't nobody got time for that.

I wonder how careful we are about agreeing to things that *really* matter—to our lives, our bodies, our hearts.

Your voice—your inner voice, too—gives life to whatever you give it to. If you don't think that what you say to yourself or to others has any bearing on your life, you are in danger. Our words and agreements work like magnets that draw us in a certain direction. Even if it's a direction we don't want to go in.

Think

Did you know that if a person talks out loud to a plant consistently, it will grow faster? Look, I didn't believe it when I first heard it either. But it's true! One study showed that plants not only grow better when talked to regularly but that a woman's voice makes a plant grow faster than a man's.[3] Okay now, ladies! Talk about girl power.

What you repeat out loud and to yourself matters. The Scriptures promise us as much! Our tongues hold the power of *life* and *death* over our careers, marriages, joy, peace, and mental health.

What has your tongue been bringing life or death to? What are some things you hear yourself saying out loud over and over again?

- "I'll be single forever."
- "All the good guys are gone."
- "I'll never get pregnant!"
- "It'll never get any better."
- "I'm just crazy."
- "I'm so stupid."
- "I always mess everything up."

Your tongue is a powerful weapon. It's up to you to decide how you use it.

Hear

Your tongue has the power of life and death.
Those who love to talk will eat the fruit of
their words.

—PROVERBS 18:21

Respond

What are some other things you find yourself "agreeing to" verbally? Refer to the list above in the "think" section as a starting point.

_____

_____

_____

_____

_____

I want to issue a challenge to you today. Every single time you come into agreement with a negative thought, even if it's in your own mind, check in with it. Pause. Think about why you're saying what you're saying. Then, immediately follow it up with positive words—and I want you to say those out loud. Trust me—it works. God's Word says it does.

Take a picture of these suggestions and open that camera roll every time your tongue is used as a weapon against you and your future.

- I am a child of God.
- I am a new creation.
- I am forgiven.
- I am inseparable from the love of God.
- Jesus Christ longs to be in a relationship with me.
- I was created on purpose, for a purpose.
- I am washed, sanctified, and justified.
- I am the very righteousness of God.
- I am fully known, fully loved, and fully accepted by God.
- God has a plan for my life. And it's better than my plan.
- I am good because God made me.

Pray

God, I pray that I would use my words to give life. Not only to myself, Lord, but to others too. I pray that the fruit of my tongue would be sweet and filling, not bitter and unsatisfying. Anytime I come into agreement with something negative, convict me. Help me to remember what's true and to say those things out loud. Amen.

DAY 23

Read

When I got engaged, it wasn't long before I began to say, "We'll never make it down the aisle." I said it over and over and over again to myself. Probably even to some other people too. I would read comments online saying my marriage was doomed, and you know what? I came into agreement with those statements.

Now, had I been checking in with myself and being honest with myself, I would have taken these thoughts captive and said, "Okay, what's really going on here?" But I wasn't being honest with myself.

Think

I am a positive person. I'm silly. I laugh a lot, and I like to make other people laugh too. I'm straight-up goofy. But when I'm not checking in with myself, I become such a Negative Nancy.

In fact, when I'm not checking in with God, myself, and others, I can be a dang fatalist. Worst-case-scenaro-ist. And it's not that I don't want good things. It's not that I don't think God wants to give me good things. But a lot of times I don't feel like I deserve good things.

So I'll guard my heart by calling a failure before it happens. And then, when something bad does happen, I am not "hurt" by it.

Only, I wonder how many good things I've spoken out of my life. How many good career opportunities, relationships, and experiences I've missed out on because I expected and looked for the worst—because I spoke the worst over and over again out loud and to myself.

Have you ever been like this? Are you like this right now? Do you look for the bad in every situation? Do you speak those thoughts out loud? Check in with that attitude, girl. Because our attitudes determine our thoughts. Our thoughts determine our words. And our words determine our futures.

Hear

The words of a man's mouth are like deep waters [copious and difficult to fathom];
    The fountain of [mature, godly] wisdom is like a bubbling stream [sparkling, fresh, pure, and life-giving].
    —PROVERBS 18:4 AMP

Respond

Today's response is going to require a little something extra from you. But if you follow through with it, it could be one of the most powerful things you do in this journal.

I want you to reach out to three people you talk to or are around regularly. Do it over text, email, or direct message. Give them some time to think before you ask for their responses, but send them these exact words:

> I am doing a study right now on checking in with God, myself, and other people. I want your honest feedback on the following three questions:
>
> 1. What is something I say a lot?
> 2. What kind of emotion do you get when I walk into a room, text, email, or call you?
> 3. What's it like to be on the other side of our relationship?

Now, don't send this to someone you already know has beef with you. Send this to people who have your best interest at heart but will also be honest with you.

Self-awareness is critical to checking in.

Pray

Father, I pray that you would help me become more aware of myself. Of my thoughts, attitudes, and words. I pray I wouldn't be a Negative Nancy. I pray I would be honest but hopeful at all times. I pray my words would be like life-giving waters—to me and to those around me. Amen.

DAY 24

Read

Do you ever find yourself saying yes when you really want to say no?

We all do this occasionally, but how many of you continually find yourself going places you don't want to go and doing things you really don't want to do?

Do you put your wants and needs on the back burner and put the needs of others first, even when it's a real inconvenience to you? Is doing something for someone else the only way you feel good about yourself?

If this is you, you may have made a spiritual agreement a while back that without works, you are worthless. You've told yourself that everybody relies on you and you can't let them down. If you do, you're selfish. So you find yourself enslaved to the demands of those around you. You're probably frustrated, drained, and feel taken advantage of.

But it's all because you haven't checked in with your motives, your *why* behind the choices you make.

Think

————

I'm about to make a confession. I've been a single lady for a minute or two now. And I know my way around a car. I can change a tire, change my own oil. You know, I'm not clueless when it comes to cars.

Only one day, I sure acted like I was.

I pulled up to the gas station to fill my tank, and my mind was a hundred different places. And I put diesel in my car instead of gasoline. Yup. I filled her right on up with the stuff. It didn't take long to figure out my mistake. I got a couple of miles down the road, and all of a sudden, *boom.* The engine just cut off.

Turns out, a gasoline engine can't run on diesel fuel.

Palm. To. Face.

But so many of us live our lives this way. Our motives—the things that keep us running—aren't adequate to keep us going forever. At least not going in a healthy way. In a sustainable way.

When you say yes to things you don't really want to do for the wrong reasons, it's like putting diesel in a car that requires gas. You can go for a little while, but eventually, *boom.* Your engine is gonna cut off.

Hear

But let your statement be, "Yes, yes" or "No, no" [a firm yes or no].

—MATTHEW 5:37 AMP

Respond

When was the last time you said yes to something you wanted to say no to? Check in with your motives. Why did you agree to do something you didn't want to do?

_____

_____

_____

_____

_____

_____

_____

_____

If you've made a spiritual agreement somewhere along the way that you're no good unless you're doing things for other people, you can release yourself from bondage—because that's what it is.

I give you permission to say no. But I'll do ya one better. *God* gives you permission to say no. Say it out loud right now. Practice it! Yell it. Sing it. It feels good, doesn't it?

What is one thing in your life that you're consistently doing that you don't want to do?

_____

_____

_____

_____

_____

_____

Put it down, sis. Set it aside. It's like diesel in your engine. And I want to see you make it to the finish line.

Pray
___

God, give me wisdom to see beyond my yeses to the motives behind my responses. Help me to weed out the yeses that should be nos. Help me to check in with my reasoning. Help me to be a person who only serves, gives to, and helps others out of love for you. Amen.

DAY 25

Read

___

Part of checking in with yourself is becoming aware of what thoughts you're having over and over again. These are usually signs of agreements you've made about yourself internally: spiritually, mentally, and emotionally.

Our minds, our thoughts, and the things we come into agreement on matter so much because they all work together to pull and push our lives in certain directions. The stakes are too high to call this thing a struggle or fight.

In other words, this is war! We have to bring every thought we have, especially thoughts we repeat over and over again, before God. If they don't line up with something he's said or reflect the love and value he has for us, then we should cast those ideas as far away from us as we can!

Bringing our thoughts to God and testing them against his Word is one of the most effective and freeing ways to check in with him.

Think

Have you ever been in a fight? Or seen one in real life? I've got a friend who is an MMA fighter, and I went to one of his matches. Y'all, I couldn't even look. They were all bloody, sweaty, and bruised up. And that was just after one round!

Let me take it a step further.

Can you imagine being in the middle of a war? A real, live, massive battle? You wouldn't walk out into that battle all casual-like with athleisure wear on, now would ya? Heck no! You'd want to be strapped up in whatever body armor you could find. You'd want to be prepared, trained, educated, and ready.

And yet, when we don't check in with the thoughts we've come into agreement on, it's like walking out to the front lines while we're digging in our purse, trying to find our phones.

That's how important it is to capture our thoughts and take them to the throne. Ask God what he thinks. Read his Word. Talk to someone who has a strong faith, and ask them their opinion. Checking in prepares you for the war. And the battlefield is right inside your own noggin.

Hear

The weapons of our warfare are not physical [weapons of flesh and blood]. Our weapons are divinely powerful for the destruction of fortresses. We are destroying sophisticated arguments and every exalted and proud thing that sets itself up against the [true] knowledge of God, and we are taking every thought and purpose captive to the obedience of Christ.

—2 CORINTHIANS 10:4–5 AMP

Respond

If you were to go into actual battle, what type of preparation would you want beforehand? What kind of weapons would you want? Information? Training? Experience?

_____

_____

_____

_____

_____

_____

_____

_____

_____

What are you doing right now to do those same things in the spiritual warfare we all face every day?

_____

_____

_____

_____

What is *one* thing you can add to your daily or weekly routine to increase your ability to win the war over your thoughts and spiritual agreements?

_____

_____

_____

_____

Pray
_____

Father, I am in an all-out war. My mind can be a worthy adversary, and I need your help to win. Help me to prepare. Help me to train. Help me to immediately recognize when I'm losing the fight with my mind. Replace any lies I've believed with your truth. Cancel out any spiritual agreements that don't line up with your Word. Thank you for lovingly leading me into battle. Amen.

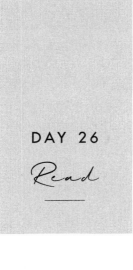

DAY 26

Read

For me, morning is when I'm the most anxious. It's like I wake up to the Enemy standing at my bedside with a tray of my mistakes for breakfast.

I've got a spoiler alert for you: while I have come so far in the checking-in process, in the end, I am still human. I have bad days. I have bad weeks even.

When I'm feeling good and checking in with myself, I can stop extreme thoughts like *It's never going to happen for me* and reason with them. But in tough weeks, it's easy to slip into that same old negative rotation of thoughts.

Think

We all have different times of day when we struggle a little bit more with anxiety and depression than others. Maybe for you it's right at bedtime. You're exhausted, you can barely keep your eyes open, and then you get in bed and all of a sudden the soundtrack of the day starts playing.

- *I shouldn't have said that.*
- *I can't believe she did that.*
- *I wonder what he* really *meant by that comment.*

That being said, numerous studies show that morning-time anxiety is very common. And there's some science behind why.

Cortisol (the stress hormone) is released by the adrenal glands in response to fear or stress. Researchers found that cortisol is at its highest level for the first hour of being awake. They even named it—the cortisol awakening response.[4]

See? You don't wake up irritable and short-tempered because you like snapping at your family or because you get a kick out of the overwhelming sense of dread that comes with your alarm clock. Why do our bodies do this? Simple—the cortisol is supposed to help us wake the heck up!

So, how can we use the cortisol awakening response to our advantage? For me, it's all about a morning routine. Now, you may say you don't have time for a morning routine, but you've already got one. It may just be a bad one.

Hear

In the morning let me hear about your
faithful love,
because I've put my trust in you.
Show me the way I should live,
because I trust you with my life.

—PSALM 143:8

Respond

Take a few minutes to write down your morning routine. Everything you do for the first hour you're awake. (Don't forget to add in the number of times you smack that snooze button, okay?)

_____

_____

_____

_____

For me, I have to start every day with prayer. Before I even get out of the bed, I spend at least five minutes talking to God and getting my mind and heart right. That doesn't have to be what you do, but within the first hour of waking up, I would suggest a check-in with the Father, even if it's just a "Yo, God.

Good morning. Thank you for another day. I'm gonna check back in with you later, but I want you to know I love you. Please lead, guide, and direct every minute of this day. Amen."

God created our bodies. The Word says that he knows when we sleep and when we rise. Our morning routine matters to God! Rewrite a new morning routine below. One that includes a check-in of some sort. Then do it!

New morning routine:

_____

_____

_____

_____

Remember: if you want to turn that morning anxiety into morning productivity, it's gonna take intentionality and consistency. So keep at it.

Pray

Father, thank you that you're a big God who still cares about the little things, like our morning routines. We all need *you* as part of those routines. Give me the determination to check in early, to invite you into every minute of each day from the very beginning. Amen.

DAY 27

Read

Saturday Night Live has always loved poking fun at me. I guess having your job performance satirized by some of the funniest people on the planet is a sideways compliment; but most days it feels really, really sideways.

You'd have to be cold, dead, and in the grave for others' perception of you to have no effect on your self-esteem. Especially when that perception is shared and perpetuated by the media.

Like I've said, I grew up with the message that I'm not worth sticking around for, that I'm not valuable or meaningful enough on my own. So, yeah. All this talk and chatter and media coverage irritated those wounds.

When Destiny's Child was at its height, these (and other) jokes about me caused an enormous amount of anxiety. *Maybe they're right. Maybe I should quit. Maybe I'm not talented. Maybe I am a joke.* Every bad thing that was said about me has echoed in my heart as truth at some point or another.

But there's a big ole problem with that. Anxiety is not a representation of truth. Anxiety is a representation of what we fear.

Think

___

Fear. Even that word sounds a little creepy, right? Makes my skin crawl!

We all have fears. Some of them are more logical than others. Like, I have this weird fear of driving across a bridge and having it collapse while I'm on it. What are the chances of that happening? Not great. But your girl will put the pedal to the metal anytime I cross one.

Then there are other types of fears, like losing a parent, that are far more likely to happen.

A third type of fear is abstract fears. The ones that spring from unhealed wounds. Like my fear that I'm not good enough. That I'm not valuable or talented. Which is just plain stupid. I mean, I was in one of the bestselling R&B groups of all time. Obviously, I got a little something going on with my voice and performance abilities.

Our fears lie to us. They whisper to us and press against those unhealed hurts and make us believe that there's some truth to them. We become anxious and insecure because it's easier to lean into our fears than it is to check in with the truth.

Hear

___

Then you will know the truth. And the truth will set you free.
—JOHN 8:32

Respond

Is there something that your family, friends, or coworkers tease you about a lot? Something that you are secretly (or not so secretly) insecure about? Bring that before God and say, "God, how much of this is truth, and how much of this is fear?"

When you hear, "Anxiety is not a representation of truth. Anxiety is a representation of what we fear," how does that change the way you view the thoughts that give you the most anxiety?

_____

_____

_____

_____

_____

_____

_____

_____

Today you can tell Satan to get outta your car and hitchhike himself right back down to the pit. You don't have to be controlled by your greatest fears. You can choose instead to lean the weight of your anxiety on the truth of who God is and who God says you are.

Pray

Father, we all have insecurities, fears, and anxieties. Some of those are rooted in wounds, and some of those are rooted in downright lies. God, convict my heart when I allow these wounds and lies to have more control over me than your truth. Remind me to check in with these thoughts—to be vigilant over them. You want me to live free from the chains of self-doubt and worry. To do that, I have to guard my heart and mind. Help me to do that today and every day. Amen.

DAY 28

Read

When we experience consistent anxiety around a thought or idea, we should check in with it and ask, "Is there any truth to this?" We shouldn't live in denial.

Because sometimes we can have *intuition*.

In my opinion, the Holy Spirit cautions us when we're about to tread somewhere we don't need to. When you enter into a relationship with Jesus, his Holy Spirit has access to lead you, guide you, comfort you, and speak to you. When I have intuitions, I believe they are given to me by the Holy Spirit.

When Chad and I got engaged, I was approached by a production company for us to do a show about our relationship. Immediately, I got a sense of foreboding dread. It felt distinctly *uncomfortable.*

And had I stopped to check in with that tug that persisted at my heart, I might have saved myself a lot of heartache. Because *that* was not meaningless anxiety. *That* was intuition—guidance from the Holy Spirit himself.

Think

Have you ever just had a bad feeling about something or someone that turned out to be right? I'm not talking about looking for the bad in every situation. I'm talking about a feeling that strikes you in the heart out of nowhere.

There's a good chance that what you were experiencing was *intuition*—a gift given to those who have a relationship with Jesus through his Holy Spirit.

I will never forget driving down the highway with my ex-fiancé one day before we agreed to do the show. We were talking about whether we should commit to it, and out of nowhere I said, "I don't feel *right* about it."

Anytime we get that little uncomfortable feeling, that whisper in our spirits, we should stop what we're doing and check in with it. Bring it to God. Line it up with his Word. Get counsel from wise friends (more on that in a couple of days).

Remember this—when you feel tension, pay attention.

Hear

But the Father will send the Friend in my name to help you. The Friend is the Holy Spirit. He will teach you all things. He will remind you of everything I have said to you.

—JOHN 14:26

Respond

Has there ever been a time in your life when you've felt the Holy Spirit lead you in a certain direction? Did you listen? What happened?

_____

_____

_____

If you have a relationship with Jesus, the Holy Spirit lives inside of you. But he's a gentleman. He ain't gonna bonk you over the head. Checking in with God, yourself, and others is the best way to sharpen the clarity of communication between you and the Holy Spirit. Invite him into your life. Ask him for wisdom and discernment in your decision-making.

According to Scripture (Isaiah 11:2–3), there are seven characteristics the Holy Spirit can give us, if we ask:

1. Wisdom
2. Understanding
3. Counsel
4. Fortitude (courage)
5. Knowledge
6. Piety (devotion to the Lord)
7. Fear of the Lord (respect for his power and greatness)

Out of the seven, which do you need most from the Holy Spirit right now?

Pray

Lord, thank you for the gift of your Holy Spirit and all you offer us through it. I ask right now that I would pay attention to the tension—any uneasiness I feel around a situation, person, or decision. I pray for all seven of the gifts of the Holy Spirit, but right now, God, I especially need _____. Thank you for giving me all I need to live in freedom and wholeness and healing. Amen.

DAY 29

Read

Sometimes a thing isn't a "good" choice or a "bad" choice; sometimes a thing is just an unwise choice.

While I felt that check in my spirit that the show wasn't "right," another side of me thought, *You've never done this before. It's just nerves. The world needs to see the ups and downs of a relationship and how to rely on God during both.* I was so sure that we wouldn't succumb to the reality TV show curse. Maybe there was a part of me that wanted to prove we were different from other couples. That our way of doing things was the "right" way.

Some of these thoughts were guilt driven. Is guilt of God? Nope.

Some of these thoughts were pride driven. What does God say about pride? It comes right before a fall.

Some of these thoughts were just plain stupid. If I had run them through the filter of common sense, I would never have agreed to the show.

Think

The thing about big life decisions is that there's rarely a glaringly "right" answer. And if you don't do your due diligence, you might make a misstep—like I did.

- This house or that house?
- Private school or public school?
- Date him or dump him?
- Take the job or turn it down?
- Say something or stay quiet?
- Move or stay?

These are all *huge* decisions that have the potential to change the trajectory of your life. And if you're not sending them all through the three filters of checking in, you could wind up with some regret.

Anytime you want to know what the Holy Spirit is trying to tell you, line up your feelings with God's Word.

If I'd have done that before signing on to the show, if I'd have checked in with that intuitive part of my mind and soul that was whispering no, I bet I would have gotten confirmation that it wasn't wise for us to do the show.

Hear

I will put my Spirit in you. I will make you want to obey my rules.
I want you to be careful to keep my laws.

—EZEKIEL 36:27

Respond

There is more than one way to test your intuition—to see if your caution in a situation is coming from the Holy Spirit. You can:

1. **Compare your intuition to God's Word.** Open your Bible or Bible app and do your research. Study Jesus' exact words and actions. Take a close look at the character of God. Those things alone will show you how our Father wants us to conduct ourselves.
2. **Pray.** Then pray again. Then pray some more. Spend more than one quiet time seeking God's wisdom. Talk to him, and pay attention to your words. Be intentional. You might be surprised by what you hear yourself saying.
3. **Seek wise counsel.** Surround yourself with people who love God and seek God. Don't ask someone for advice unless you'd like your life to look like theirs.

4. **Create time to hear from God.** We're so busy coming and going that we rarely create "empty space" in our minds to receive God's voice. Take a walk without your earbuds in. Listen to instrumental worship music. Sit in silence in a quiet room. Ask God to speak to you, and listen to what you hear.

5. **Journal.** Writing out my thoughts is the way that I best hear from the Holy Spirit. Whenever I feel like the Holy Spirit is trying to communicate with me, I open the notepad app on my phone and write down exactly what I'm thinking, feeling, and sensing. Getting what's inside of us *outside of us* sometimes brings a whole new revelation.

Out of the five ways to check in with the Holy Spirit, which do you need to work on the most?

_____

How can you begin to make checking in that way a habit? Be specific in your response.

_____

_____

_____

_____

_____

_____

_____

Pray

Heavenly Father, I want to hear from your Holy Spirit. I don't want to make any missteps. Let your voice be the loudest voice in my ears, mind, and heart. I want your perfect will— nothing less. Help me to check in with you in a way that makes it abundantly clear what I need to do in any given situation. Thank you for leading me. Amen.

DAY 30

Read

One of the biggest differences between anxiety and intuition is the way they make you feel. Since intuition is from God, it should leave you feeling a little more relaxed, a little more at peace. But anxiety? Anxiety is not of God. I personally think anxiety is from the pit of hell. And it comes on you like a cold grip around your heart, making you feel nauseous, panicky, and unsure.

For example, when I was in the car and said the words "I don't feel right about this," they just fell out of my mouth. And I felt better after saying those words out loud.

Anxiety is unsettling. It feels like an anchor dragging our very being into a pit of dark despair. But intuition? Intuition will feel "pleasant" to your soul. Not great, but pleasant. Intuition ain't gonna make you jump for joy. But it will feel quietly true, and truth brings peace and rest.

Think

Why is it that we'll get married to anxiety but we tell our intuition to shut its mouth and go to bed without supper?

For one, it's hard to know the difference until you're on the wrong side of an unwise choice. Sometimes when we trust our gut, we end up believing it's a good idea to call in sick to work, eat ice cream straight out of the tub, and not leave the house all day.

Anxiety robs many of us of the ability to check in with that inner intuitive voice—the voice of the Holy Spirit, the voice of God.

So, how do we know the difference?

Ask yourself the following questions about your gut feeling:

- Is this feeling rooted in fear? (Anxiety is rooted in fear. Intuition is rooted in wisdom.)
- How does this make me feel emotionally? Slightly relaxed (intuition)? Or highly panicked (anxiety)?
- How does this make me feel physically? Not much change (intuition)? Or increased heart rate, stomach pains, and restlessness (anxiety)?
- How *intensely* do I feel this? (Anxiety is more intense than intuition.)
- How much pressure do I feel when I think this? (Anxiety is more demanding than intuition.)

If you give yourself the space to think through these questions, you'll be far more likely to lean on intuition and kick anxiety to the curb.

Hear

For the LORD gives [skillful and godly] wisdom;
From His mouth come knowledge and
    understanding.
He stores away sound wisdom for the righteous
    [those who are in right standing with Him];
He is a shield to those who walk in integrity
    [those of honorable character and moral
    courage],
He guards the paths of justice;
And He preserves the way of His saints
    (believers).
Then you will understand righteousness and
    justice [in every circumstance]
And integrity and every good path.
For [skillful and godly] wisdom will enter your
    heart
And knowledge will be pleasant to your soul.

—PROVERBS 2:6–10 AMP

Respond

Think about a decision you have to make soon. Maybe it's today. Tomorrow. Next week. A year from now. What's your gut feeling about that decision?

_____

_____

_____

_____

_____

Now look back at the questions from the "think" section. Answer them below as they pertain to your gut feeling.

_____

_____

_____

_____

After your assessment, would you say your gut feeling is a response to anxiety or intuition?

_____

_____

_____

_____

Pray

God, thank you for giving me so many different ways to make sure I'm using wisdom to make the best choices for me and for my family. I pray that, as I move forward, you would help me become better and better at picking out your voice among all the scattered noise in my head. Amen.

DAY 31

Read

I went public with my depression by accident.

In 2013 I was doing a round of media, and before I knew it, I was talking about how the prior year had been a very difficult one for me because I had struggled with depression.

Once I said it, I was like, *Oh my gosh, what did I just say?* But once I had released those words into the universe, there was no catching them and shoving them back in.

Not long after that, I did *Good Morning America* for that same round of media. An older man pulled me to the side with tears in his eyes right there in the studio. And he thanked me profusely. He thanked me for talking about my depression publicly, for giving the world a point of reference for all those who suffer in silence.

I encouraged him to get help, and I told him that he wasn't alone.

Think

You know one of the Enemy's favorite things to whisper to us?

You're the only one. You're all alone in this. No one can relate to you.

Satan likes to isolate us because that makes us easier targets for further destruction. Just like God has a plan for you, the Enemy has a plan as well. And we've gotta be checking in to make sure we're following the right one. To make sure we're embracing truth and not drowning in lies.

So if you're feeling alone in something right now, know this—you are *never* alone. God is with you. God is for you. And as long as you can hang on to that knowledge, Satan doesn't stand a chance.

Hear

Here is what I am commanding you to do. Be strong and brave. Do not be afraid. Do not lose hope. I am the LORD your God. I will be with you everywhere you go.

—JOSHUA 1:9

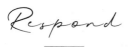

Respond

When is a time in your life that you felt alone? When you felt like you were the "only one" in your circumstances or situation? How did you handle those thoughts and feelings?

_____

_____

_____

_____

_____

Now that you know more about checking in, would you have done anything differently?

_____

_____

_____

_____

_____

The next time you start believing the lie that you're "the only one," I want you to stop whatever you're doing and check in with the truth of God's promise never to leave you or forsake you. Then tell the devil to get behind you. Say it out loud, sis! And walk in the freedom of knowing that you are never, never alone.

Pray

God, your Word tells me to be strong and brave—not to be afraid or to lose hope. Actually, it commands me to be those things. But I can't do that without you. That's why you also promise to be with me wherever I go. There's no place, no pit, no feeling, and no thought that I must face alone. Thank you for loving me so fiercely, God. Amen.

DAY 32

Read

The topic of my depression came up again when I was on *The Talk* in 2017. In that interview, I actually went further to say that I had experienced suicidal thoughts. Again, I hadn't planned on saying that, but I did.

But you know what? Once again, I experienced this incredible response of, "Thank you. You showed me I'm not the only one. You taught me I can overcome this. You inspired me to talk to someone about how I'm feeling."

The more I've shared, the more people in my life and around me have been able to share too.

Think

Maybe you're not clinically depressed. Maybe you are. Maybe you just have moments of anxiety that leave you feeling shaky and on edge. Or maybe you have a diagnosis and take medication.

Wherever you are in your journey of mental health, I would encourage you to be honest about it. The more people share their truth openly, the more other people feel permission to share theirs.

I'm not saying you've gotta post a picture of your bottle of antidepressants on social media. I'm just saying that when you are given the opportunity to share, do it.

God wants to leverage your pain for *good*. I mean, isn't that what God is all about? Using anything and everything he can to draw his people to him?

It's time to deconstruct the stigma that people who experience challenges with their mental health are broken. Nah. We ain't broken. In fact, we're some of the strongest people on the planet because we fight a battle every day inside our own bodies—the place we're supposed to feel safest.

Own your story. Then, give it away. You may be the very reason someone else starts checking in with theirs.

Hear

But he said to me, "My grace is all you need. My power is strongest when you are weak." So I am very happy to brag about how weak I am. Then Christ's power can rest on me.

—2 CORINTHIANS 12:9

Respond

Talking about our weaknesses is not something our culture encourages, is it? But sharing our stories with one another—openly and honestly—is one way we can both help others and find power with admission through Christ.

But first you have to be honest with yourself about where your mental health is right now. Go on. Brag about those weaknesses for a hot minute.

_____

_____

_____

_____

_____

_____

_____

_____

_____

_____

_____

Now that you've been honest with yourself, how can you share your story with others who may need to hear it?

Pray

Heavenly Father, your Word says that you are strongest when I am at my weakest. And nothing feels weaker than admitting my greatest inner struggles out loud. But Lord, I also know that there is freedom in the vulnerability of sharing my story. Give me the courage to share and the wisdom to share appropriately, knowing that the response I get is something you will take care of in your own way, on your own time. Amen.

DAY 33

Read

After I got engaged, I'm sure I was the picture of bliss and excitement. What no one knew was that my depression was raging.

Now, my ex knew about my past struggles with mental health, but he didn't know I was in full-blown active depression again. I didn't say anything to anybody because I didn't want people to be like, *Oh Lord! Here we go again.* I definitely didn't want my new fiancé to be questioning whether I was stable enough to be his wife.

He'd never known me to be fully depressed, and I wanted to keep it that way. So, for about seven months, I was faking it.

Think

You've probably heard the saying "Fake it till you make it," right? Now, that little adage works well in some scenarios, but when it comes to most, it's a surefire way to screw up.

Think about it. What if you faked it till you made it when you were cooking? You think your family is gonna eat burned chicken and not let you know just how foul it tastes? No. They'll let you know that they can straight up tell you were faking your culinary skills.

The same is true when we try to fake our emotions for too long. Despite our best efforts, other people will soon be able to tell how we're *really* feeling. We can't keep them from noticing the charred aftertaste of our darker emotions.

Hear

So we can say boldly,
"The Lord helps me. I will not be afraid.
What can mere human beings do to me?"
—HEBREWS 13:6

Respond

In what area of your life are you "faking it till you make it"?

_____

_____

_____

There's an expiration date on anything we're stuffing down, hiding, or covering up. Sooner or later the truth always comes out. How can you become more honest about the ways you're faking it right now?

_____

_____

_____

_____

_____

_____

_____

_____

_____

_____

Pray

_____

God, you care about authenticity. But more than that, you care about *me*. You want me to live wholly and healed. And I can never get there by being fake. I can never get there until I admit that I'm struggling. That I need help—that I need *you*. Give me the strength to let go of others' perceptions and be real. That's what you desire from me and for me. I love you. Amen.

DAY 34

Read

As Chad and I prepared to merge our households, I moved from my hometown in Illinois to the West Coast—LA.

Once I got settled there, I could see the disease of depression beginning to infect random places in my life.

For example, I couldn't bring myself to buy furniture for my place. I just didn't have the desire to do it. Which is so unlike me—I love decorating and making places homey. But for some reason (ahem, depression), I didn't have the energy to do the things I used to love.

I told myself I was just sad that I had to downsize so much. That it was normal to experience some feelings of grieving and sadness when you move. That I missed my family, the cornfields, and the small town I had left.

No one is a better liar than a depressed person in denial.

Think

Our minds are powerful things, y'all. So powerful, in fact, that they can convince us that certain things are true or untrue as a defense mechanism. Like denial.

Denial happens anytime we refuse to accept our current reality.

If we're riding in a car together and the stoplight is red, but I turn to you and say, "The light turned green," and I start driving, you're going to want to grab the wheel, right? That's what denial is. It's the same thing as looking at a red light and calling it green.

- We refuse to admit that we're in a toxic relationship that needs to end.
- We refuse to admit that we're in over our heads and overwhelmed.
- We refuse to admit that even though we act like we've got it together, inside we're a total mess.

If checking in had a complete opposite, it would be denial.

When we deny ourselves or those closest to us the truth, it's the same as living a lie. A reckless lie that could end in a catastrophic crash.

Hear

___

Don't lie to one another. You have gotten rid of your old way
of life and its habits.

—COLOSSIANS 3:9

Respond

___

Denial is just one of the defense mechanisms we use to guard
ourselves and others from feeling exposed, vulnerable, guilty,
or ashamed. Here are a few others:[5]

MECHANISM	DESCRIPTION
Repression	Works to keep thoughts out of our conscious awareness
Projection	Takes our own feelings, thoughts, and actions and assigns them to other people
Rationalization	Explains our behaviors or feelings in a logical way, ignoring the true reasons behind them
Regression	Reverts to old patterns of behavior when confronted with stress
Denial	Blocks facts, feelings, and thoughts from our awareness as a refusal to experience them

Looking at the chart, which of the defense mechanisms do you use most often in times of stress, anxiety, or depression?

_____

_____

_____

_____

Instead of ignoring what's already true, we have the choice to check in. We have the choice to be honest. Honesty gets us what we want in the end—relief from our pain. How can you be more honest when you really want to hide what you're going through?

_____

_____

_____

_____

Pray
___

Heavenly Father, your Word talks a lot about honesty. But I've been conditioned to hide anything that makes me appear to be different or imperfect. God, convict me anytime I replace checking in with a coping mechanism. Show me how to open up and who to open up to. And remind me to start with you. Amen.

DAY 35

Read

In our relationship, Chad was a "fixer." He would swoop in and save the day. He was good at figuring out what needed to be done and doing it. Unfortunately, you can't "save" someone from depression.

Especially when you don't even know that's what the person you love is suffering from. And in the state I was in, I couldn't remove myself enough emotionally to see that he was trying to help me. Instead, it felt like he was patronizing me.

I would get so irritated when he offered support. He'd be like, "Let me make a call. Let me scramble some eggs. Let me handle this meeting." And I'd hear, "You can't get it together. See what I have to deal with? I have to do all this *for* you because you're incapable of doing it alone."

Think

___

Not many things make me madder than someone thinking I can't do something on my own. I'm an independent person, and I'm proud of the fact that I find completion in God and God alone.

That's why I stink at receiving help. I mean, I'm bad at it. When I go to a restaurant, I almost feel guilty. Like, "Lemme take these dishes back to the kitchen. I got this."

It's silly. It's pride.

When the people around us notice that we're in a state of need and try (in their own way) to meet that need, it can feel demeaning. It can feel shameful.

Did you catch that, though? It can *feel.* Our feelings aren't always fact. The fact is, we all need help at some point in our lives. And if we aren't open to that, we aren't living out God's commandment to share one another's burdens. And we make it harder for other people to accept help when they need it too.

Hear

___

Carry one another's heavy loads. If you do, you will fulfill the law of Christ.

—GALATIANS 6:2

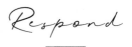

Respond

When was the last time you asked someone for help in a way that made you feel vulnerable?

_____

_____

_____

_____

_____

If you can't think of a time, then we've got a problem.

What's one area, situation, or task that you really need help with right now?

_____

_____

_____

_____

_____

_____

I want to challenge you to send a text, make a call, or write an email to someone you trust and ask them to help you. Maybe it's as simple as asking someone to pray. Maybe it's as daunting as making an appointment with a counselor. Whatever it is, do it. And do it now!

Pray

God, it's easy for most of us to offer help when we see
someone in need. It's a lot harder to accept help when it's
offered to us. Search my heart, Lord. Remove any pride that
is within me. Remind me that you created people to be in
community together—to serve one another and to carry one
another's heavy loads. Give me the grit to say those three
magnificently powerful words out loud: "I need help." Amen.

DAY 36

Read

Imagine that my mind is a big electric fan.

On a good day, it whirls to life perfectly at the highest set-ting, humming right along as I go about life. On a hard day, it's like a fan on a lower setting. I'm still getting the job done, but it takes a lot more time and effort. On my worst days, the fan has an electrical short. I keep plugging it in and unplugging it. Sometimes it'll huff and puff a few times, but others, no luck.

Think

As believers, we're often taught to check in with our spiritual wellness. How's your heart? How's your soul? How close do you feel to God right now? Those are important questions—life-giving questions that we should all be asking ourselves regularly.

But there are other questions that matter too. For those of us suffering with a diagnosed mental health illness, and for people who experience occasional to frequent anxiety or depression, there are important questions to consider:

- Have I been more worried or anxious than normal lately?
- Have I been getting quality sleep with regular sleep and wake times?
- Have I felt more sad than glad lately?
- Have I been isolating myself at work, at home, or from friends?
- Have I been having trouble concentrating or getting what I need to get done, done?
- Do I have an appetite? Have my eating habits changed recently?

We all—and I mean *allll*—need to do frequent mental health check-ins. Our hearts, souls, spirits? Yes, they all matter. But our minds matter as well.

Hear

Then God's peace will watch over your hearts and your minds. He will do this because you belong to Christ Jesus. God's peace can never be completely understood.

—PHILIPPIANS 4:7

Respond

Why don't we do a mental health check-in right now?

_____ On a scale of 1 to 10, what has your anxiety level been lately (1 being the least anxious, 10 being the most anxious)?

_____ On a scale of 1 to 10, what has your depression level been the last few days (1 being the least depressed you've ever felt, 10 being the most depressed you've ever felt)?

Ask yourself the questions listed above in the "think" section. Then, consider your answers. Check in with the truth that they represent.

Pray

Father, thank you for caring about my mental wellness. Thank you for the doctors, medications, and tools available to me. Help me to embrace the truth that it's okay not to be okay sometimes. You have made a way for me to be my best self through earthly resources as well as prayer and spiritual disciplines. I pray for spiritual _and_ mental peace. Your peace. The peace that only you can give. Amen.

DAY 37

Read

During my engagement, I was out of it. In my head, I viewed everything through the filter of *This wedding isn't happening anyway because he is going to leave me or not fight for me. So I should end this thing before he does.*

What had Chad ever done to make me think for one second that he would leave me? I didn't have a good answer. But it got to the point where every time we had an argument, I felt like he didn't love me anymore. This started happening a lot. And I mean *a lot.* I felt unworthy of receiving what I'd prayed for.

There were so many seeds of doubt planted in my mind. From my past, from the Enemy, from myself. And in my mind, I came into agreement with those doubts, repeating them to myself over and over again. Every time I told myself the relationship was doomed, I watered those seeds until I had this big ole lavish garden of doubt in full bloom.

Think

Raise your hand if you are really, really good at self-sabotaging. Go on. I don't care if you're in a cute little coffee shop or at home in your bed. Raise that hand!

One common characteristic of people who aren't checking in is that we are awesome at convincing ourselves everyone is out to get us and every situation has the potential to bring us down. We'll have something great put right on our doorstep and kick it to the curb like it's last week's garbage.

At the root of our actions is usually a deep sense of unworthiness. A deep sense that we don't deserve good things. A deep sense that if we do accept a gift or blessing, we'll have to "pay for it" with a disappointment down the road.

The thing is, if we got what we *actually* deserved as imperfect, human sinners, our lives and ultimate futures would look a lot different. Instead, Christ gave his life for us.

And we ignore that truth when we use our words, thoughts, and actions to steer our lives away from happiness, joy, and peace. All because we're not checking in.

Hear

But here is how God has shown his love for us. While we were still sinners, Christ died for us.

—ROMANS 5:8

Respond

When's the last time you self-sabotaged? Or a time you received something from God but couldn't enjoy it because you felt undeserving?

_____

_____

_____

_____

_____

What words, actions, or thoughts led to the self-sabotage?

_____

_____

_____

_____

Do you believe you deserve good things now? Why or why not? Go back and look at today's scripture before responding.

_____

_____

_____

_____

_____

Pray

God, you sent your Son, Jesus, to live a perfect life and die a shameful death—all for us. Help me to see myself the way you see me. Help me to accept the good gifts you want to give me. Remind me that checking in is one of the best ways I can avoid self-sabotage. I love you! Amen.

DAY 38

Read

By the time that following summer hit, I was completely bugging out. I just remember feeling like I was in complete darkness. I felt ashamed, lonely, and misunderstood. I was lost. I knew I needed a reset, but I didn't know how to do that.

I was sitting in the hair and makeup chair on the set of a show I was filming, and the sweet little makeup artist could tell I was not okay. She was like, "Honey, what is going on?"

So I opened up to her and told her what I was going through. She shared with me her own struggle with anxiety, and it really touched me that she was so vulnerable.

But listening to her also made me realize something very important. The current state of my anxiety and depression was far, far worse than the average person's.

Think

Have you ever realized something about yourself that you just didn't want to accept?

- Maybe you realized you're a bad cook.
- Maybe you realized you're prone to gossip.
- Maybe you realized you can be a little lazy and sometimes procrastinate.

When I first realized my depression had returned, I was in denial. Then, after I accepted the fact that my depression had returned, I was paralyzed. I didn't know what to do next. So, I did nothing.

And lemme tell you—*nothing* is the absolute worst thing you can do when you see that something about your life, your character, or your mental health needs to change.

We all do this, right? We know we need to shed a few pounds, but we do nothing. We know we need to ask for forgiveness from someone, but we do nothing. We know we need to do *something*, but we do *nothing*.

That's because taking the first step is hard. We can live in our heads all day long—scheming of ways to get better and do better. But until we take an active approach to improvement, it's the same as doing—you guessed it—nothing.

Hear

Now you know these things. So you will be blessed if you do them.

—JOHN 13:17

Respond

Identify two or three areas in your life where you need to take a first step in improving, and make a list of them.

_____

_____

_____

_____

The first step is always the hardest. But immense relief is sure to follow it. Looking back at your list, write down what a first step toward healing and wholeness and health would be for each item.

_____

_____

_____

_____

Now it's time for another challenge. Don't worry, y'all! I'm doing these same things in my own life. I know some of this stuff is tough. I want you to circle *one* of the things from your "could improve on" list. And I want you to complete that first step in the next seven days.

You *can* do it. One small step at a time.

Pray

God, even your Word differentiates between *knowing* something and *doing* something. And you promise that I will be blessed by turning my knowledge into action. Father, make me aware of any area, relationship, or situation in my life that requires my attention. Uncover my blind spots so that I may see what I can improve on. Then give me the courage to take that first step. Amen.

DAY 39

Read

I knew I was depressed, and I also knew I needed to do something about it. But I didn't.

Not long after my random confession to the sweet makeup artist, my entire life erupted.

Chad and his nephews came to visit me, but I felt inadequate to host them. I didn't love my apartment. I don't cook. I was overly sensitive, and we ended up having a blowout argument.

Like a shaken-up bottle of champagne, your girl popped like a cork. I had said some pretty hurtful things to Chad along the way, but that visit, I got nasty.

Think

Have you ever said something you wished you could take back? Ever shoved your foot so far in your mouth that you wound up tap dancing on your larynx? Well, I sure have. More than once. But during that visit, it was like I wasn't even in control of my own tongue.

The dangers of not checking in regularly and honestly are many, but one of the greatest risks we take is wounding those we love most.

You've heard the saying "Hurt people hurt people." Usually, sayings are sayings because there's a lot of truth to them. And this one is no exception.

I hurt someone I loved deeply because I was aching inside. Maybe you, too, have done something like this:

- Maybe you got into an argument with a friend, and now you don't speak.
- Maybe you threw a cutting insult at a family member, and the weight of your words still hangs between the two of you.
- Or maybe you just went silent in a relationship, and that silence has continued.

When we are hurting, and that hurt persists and we do nothing about it, chances are we *will* hurt someone else.

Sister, learn from my regret. The price I paid for my pride was far, far too high.

Hear

My wounds are ugly. They stink.
I've been foolish. I have sinned.

—PSALM 38:5

Respond

Have *you* ever been hurt by someone who was hurting? What happened? How did that make you feel?

_____

_____

_____

_____

_____

Turn the tables. When have you wounded someone because of your own pain?

_____

_____

_____

_____

_____

Is it possible for you to bring healing to that situation? Is it possible for you to check in with yourself and determine where you were at fault? Can you make a call? Send a letter, email, text?

Asking for forgiveness may seem silly at this point, but you never know how many of your words are still echoing in the heads of those you've spoken them to.

Pray
___

God, I ask forgiveness for any time I've hurt people when I was hurting. My wounds are *my* responsibility. You tell me that I can bring them to you for healing. And that's what I'd like to do right now. I pray for wholeness through you. I pray for healing through you. I pray for restoration through you. And, if there's someone I need to ask for forgiveness from, make me brave enough to do that today. Amen.

DAY 40

Read

My relationship was over. As soon as I realized what had happened, the bottom fell out for me. I spent the next couple of days on my sofa, vacillating between catatonic and hysterical.

In fact, it had gotten so bad that all I could think about was dying. If I ceased to exist, then I wouldn't have to feel the way I was feeling anymore. The thoughts of suicide I was having were dangerous.

One night my pastor friend and his wife called me.

"We know *you*," they told me. "This isn't *you*. You are a child of a King! You are dearly loved and cherished."

Someone mentioned me checking myself in somewhere. And I knew that was probably the best idea because what I was doing wasn't working anymore. I decided to sleep on it. When I woke up the next morning, I knew it deep down in my bones. No matter how embarrassing or inconvenient or dang expensive it was going to be, it was time to check myself in somewhere.

And that check-in was one of the most important check-ins of my entire life.

Think

One of my biggest fears in life is letting down the people who depend on me. But sometimes we have to fail others for a season so we can make a long-term win for ourselves.

When I decided to check into a hospital, I was in the middle of filming a TV spot for *Raven's Home*. That meant a lot of people showing up to work on a lot of days were not able to do their jobs because I wasn't there. I think they had to reshoot the entire episode.

Talk about disappointing people.

But you know what? Taking care of yourself is something you can't afford to skip. It's something that may feel uncomfortable, may be inconvenient, and may even be embarrassing at the time. But ultimately, it gives people a better version of you.

When Jesus and his disciples were traveling and teaching throughout the Nazarene villages, Jesus noticed that his friends needed to rest. He even told them to go take a nap (Mark 6:31)! If Jesus and the disciples could take a break from spreading the gospel, you can take a break from whatever it is you're doing.

Hear

But many people were coming and going. So they did not even have a chance to eat. Then Jesus said to his apostles, "Come with me by yourselves to a quiet place. You need to get some rest."

—MARK 6:31

Respond

How long has it been since you did any of the following:

- Got eight, uninterrupted hours of sleep
- Went on a vacation (without kids, for you mamas)
- Talked to a pastor, counselor, or mentor
- Took a few days off from work
- Got your hair done
- Exercised
- Read a book or watched a movie of your choosing
- Bought something that was just for you
- Spent quality time with friends

If your answer to any of those is longer than a few months, you need to check in with yourself by taking care of yourself.

Choose at least one of those items listed and put it on your schedule. Then, follow through with it!

Investing in yourself *is also* an investment in those you love. Give them the best you. Give *you* the best you.

Pray

Heavenly Father, you have designed us to be people who rely on one another. Having people depend on us is a good thing. But when we allow people to lean on us at the expense of our mental and physical health, it steals our joy. Help me to recognize when it's okay to let people down. Help me to take care of the body and mind that you have given me so that I can live out your complete and perfect will for me. Amen.

DAY 41

Read

Before I could talk myself out of it, I got in my car and drove myself to the facility. That drive was a blur. I just threw on a sweat suit and a hat and went. I didn't pack a single thing.

Once inside the hospital, that frenzied, manic energy that had gotten me there evaporated. It was like I had been dog-paddling in the middle of the ocean for a week and I was finally on shore, able to catch my breath. I felt safe for the first time since I could remember.

There were so many brilliant people inside the facility. It wasn't like what you see in the movies: a bunch of drugged-up people wearing white, shuffling around like zombies. These people had stories and souls. These people mattered to God.

Think

How many times have we put people in culturally defined boxes before we got to know them—the real them? I know I'm guilty of it. Our stereotypes and biases are so ingrained that we don't even know when we're judging people.

Sometimes I wonder what it would be like if we all treated everybody like they mattered to God. Because, well—they do.

- That weird dude you can't stand in your office? He matters to God.
- That annoying girl who posts thirty-seven selfies a day? She matters to God.
- That group of people you automatically feel repulsion toward? They matter to God.

Everyone matters to God.

Mental illness is highly stigmatized in our society—and in the church. In general, when someone scrounges up the courage to admit they've been struggling with finding joy and peace, everybody in the church gets reeeeeeaaaaaaaal quiet. Add on top of that suicidal ideations and you'll find yourself sitting alone for a fiery hot minute.

Because we're supposed to be grateful, right? We're supposed to be manifesting the fruit of the Spirit, which includes a sound mind, right?

I don't have all the answers, but I do know this: everyone matters to God. The guilty, the forgotten, the marginalized, and the poor. Everyone matters to God—the mentally ill included.

Hear

All of us have one Father. One God created us. So why do we break the covenant the LORD made with our people of long ago? We do this by being unfaithful to one another.

—MALACHI 2:10

Respond

Get ready to check in with some thoughts and feelings that *may* make you a little uncomfortable.

Who is someone (a person or a group of people) you just don't like? They haven't done anything to you directly, but they just make your skin crawl?

How does hearing that they matter to God change the way you view them, if at all?

_____

_____

_____

_____

Can you dig down deep? Can you examine your heart and ask God to remove any judgments or partiality you may hold for certain people? Can you treat everyone like they matter to God?

Pray

Father, I ask forgiveness for any time I have put someone in a box or category prematurely. Search me, God, and find any biases that I may hold against a person, gender, race, or group of people. Reveal those to me so that I can work on these character defects. So I can love my neighbors like you've asked me to. Help me to always treat others like they matter to you—because they do. Amen.

DAY 42

Read

I had only been out of the hospital for a couple of weeks when I learned that, legally, Chad and I had to start back filming our reality TV show.

So I had a new dilemma. Should we allow my stay in the hospital to become part of the story line—or not?

I had people in my ear again, people telling me I *should* share.

Had I been in a healthier position, I would have asked myself, *Now, are these folks who are bending your ear folks who know you, love you, and want the best for you?*

The answer would have informed how much influence I allowed these "other" voices to have. But I never gauged the motives of those around me. I wasn't checking in with who I was checking in with.

Think

I've got a girlfriend who had this funky, vintage orange sofa that she took with her to every house or apartment she lived in for years and years. She'd always complain about it.

"This thing is so uncomfortable. This thing is so old and beat up. This thing is so hard to decorate around!"

One day, I was like, "Girl. If this couch gives you that much grief, why don't you just get a new one?"

She shrugged. "I don't know. It's just always been around."

If you think about it, we do the same thing she did in situations where the risk is much higher than a sore back or booty. We do this in our relationships with friends.

We stay in relationships with people because they've "always been around." We never stop to check in with whether the relationship is healthy. It's like that ugly orange couch. We look at it and don't have the energy to make a change.

Instead, we shift our perspectives, our beliefs, and our actions based on people who may not even want what's best for us. Not that they're out to get us—I think this is rarely the case. But are we getting counsel from people whose lives reflect a life we'd want for ourselves?

When we don't check in with who we're checking in with, we put our entire futures at risk.

Hear

Walk with the wise and become wise,
for a companion of fools suffers harm.
—PROVERBS 13:20 NIV

Respond

When you have a problem, conflict, or just feel stuck, who is the first person you call? The second? Third? Make a list of the people whose advice you take into account when you're making a difficult decision. Be honest with yourself. This is *so* important.

_____

_____

_____

_____

Take a look at your list. Put a star by anyone whose life, relationships, and faith reflect what you want for yourself.

This is your A-team, sis. These are the people you should be checking in with. Now, I'm not saying we have to go ending relationships with the other folks. I'm just telling you that we should be very careful about who we go to for advice and counsel.

Pray

Lord, you created us to be people who need community. Like your Word says, as iron sharpens iron, we become better because of the people around us. At the same time, we can also suffer because of the people around us. Help me to iden-tify the wise people in my circle and to rely on you first and them second when I have to make difficult decisions. Amen.

DAY 43

Read

When the reality show cameras started running again, they caught us at what was then our very lowest.

Needless to say, the relationship was stressed. *Stressed* isn't even a good word, actually. We were crumbling, splintering at the breaking point.

I personally needed to heal too. I wasn't going to be good for anybody until I addressed my mental health directly.

But here were some very real fears roaring between my ears. I was worried about my life. I was worried about my career. I had already dipped out to go to the hospital; if I did go through the legal process required to quit the show, would I ever be seen as trustworthy in the industry again?

See, when you check in with others, you can't just listen to what's being said to you and take it as the right thing to do. You've got to ask yourself, *Is this wise?* You've got to ask God, *What does your Word say? What does the Holy Spirit tell me about this?* Running it through all three filters of checking in will give you the clearest, most rounded, and fullest view of which choices to make and which to avoid.

Think

Filters. We use them for our coffee and our water. We use a filter when we talk to certain people and have to choose our words carefully. Heck, we even use them for our selfies. But when it comes to making tough choices, to hearing from God, we'll just kinda "go with the flow" or do whatever is easiest at the moment. We don't use a filter.

But that's what checking in is—three filters we should be using consistently. Not just when a problem arises, but daily. Checking in is a lifestyle.

There's a dude in the Bible named Solomon. In 1 Kings we learn that Solomon made a sacrifice to God, so God appeared to him in a dream and asked him what he wanted in return. Solomon could have said eternal youth, all the gold in the kingdom, or the fastest, coolest-looking donkey to ride around on. But Solomon asked for wisdom (3:1–15).

Solomon knew that wisdom is one of the most valuable currencies we can have. And checking in with *all* three ways is the very best way for us to gain it.

Hear

Trust in the LORD with all your heart
and lean not on your own understanding;
in all your ways submit to him,
and he will make your paths straight.

—PROVERBS 3:5–6 NIV

Respond

I start each day by checking in with God. Even if it's just a few minutes, I'm talking to God as soon as my eyelids open. Then I check in with myself. What do I need to get done? Is there anything ahead that gives me anxiety? How can I love on others? How can I love on myself? I take a quick mental, emotional, and spiritual inventory. At some point during the day, I check in with my close friends—even if it's just a quick text. These are the people I have sought out and created relationships with because they are *good* for me. I have given them full permission to ask me hard things and say hard things to me because I want and need accountability in my life. Because I trust they love God. Because I know they are wise. Then I end each day by spending more time with God. Again, maybe it's just a quick prayer. If I haven't yet, I make sure I read his Word and do a little studying.

The three filters of checking in, when repeated in a

pattern that works for you, provide the ultimate lifestyle guide for anyone seeking wholeness and healing.

How can you make checking in a lifestyle? Write down your own ideas and practices below.

_____

_____

_____

_____

_____

_____

_____

_____

_____

_____

Pray

_____

Father, I want to be a wise person because I know that using wisdom protects me, guides me, and gets me inside your perfect will. Help me to make checking in a lifestyle. Something that becomes so much a part of who I am that I begin to do it automatically. Amen.

DAY 44

Read

___

I probably prayed more during that time than I ever have in my entire life. But I wasn't getting better, and I didn't feel like I knew what to do next.

Discerning God's will isn't always easy. There have been times when he has spoken to me so clearly that I'd bet my life on it. Then there are times it feels like I'm begging him for just a gentle nudge in one direction, and all I get is silence.

But that's where faith comes in. That's where relying on intuition, that knowledge that feels like it's always been there because it's from the Holy Spirit, comes in. And to be honest, I think God is okay with us wrestling with our own thoughts every once in a while. That's what makes us grow.

Think

You know what's annoying? The silent treatment. That's why people do it—as a punishment. So when we perceive God as being silent, how are we supposed to interpret that?

If you read in the Old Testament, you'll see some of the great prophets had these same struggles. Even David, the man after God's own heart, got frustrated with God. In the opening to Psalm 13, David was like, "Hey God! Remember me? How long do you plan on ignoring me? Are you thinking forever? Because I'm straight-up wrestling with my own thoughts over here, and I could really use your help!" (my paraphrase).

Did God hear David? Yes. Did God love David? Yes.

Does God hear us? Yes. Does God love us? Yes.

So we can only believe that when we don't hear a clear answer from God, he is staying silent out of love. Out of knowing our next steps even though we don't.

And even though it frustrates us, hurts us, and sometimes scares us, God is comfortable with our discomfort. Because, like any loving parent, God wants us to be the best versions of ourselves. And he knows that through allowing us to squirm a little, we grow. Whether we fail or succeed, we *learn*.

Hear

But if he remains silent, who can judge him?

—JOB 34:29

Respond

Have you ever prayed about something—maybe prayed a whole lot—and received silence in return? How did it make you feel? How did you respond?

_____

_____

_____

_____

_____

Knowing that God hears us and loves us, what reason(s) do you think he had for being silent in that situation? What did you learn? How did you grow?

_____

_____

_____

_____

_____

Pray

Heavenly Father, I know you want good things for me. But more than that, you want good *in* me. You are shaping me and molding me into the person you created me to be. And sometimes that means you are silent when I pray. Help me to be patient. To read your Word and check in with wise counsel in these moments. Help me to have faith that silence is sometimes the best answer you can give. I love you, Lord. Amen.

DAY 45

Read

Since 2018 I have been way more intentional about my circle. I have had to get out and actually *look* for awesome friends instead of relying on life to provide friends for me. That means I've had to get uncomfortable at times. I've had to go to events and talk to people I didn't know. I've had to slide into other women's DMs to try and be their friend.

Some of my deepest friendships have been ones that I've sought out. I've looked for people in the next season of life from me. I've looked for people who are something I aspire to be. I've looked for people who have things that I want. Not necessarily material things, but spiritual things. Character traits I want to possess. Emotional stability. Honesty.

It matters who you are checking in with. It could be the determining factor in whether you reach your full potential.

Think

We've talked a lot about the people we are checking in with. We've said we need to assess the people who are in our lives by chance—those who have "always been around." But what we haven't talked about is how to *find* people to check in with.

That's right. One more thing you gotta do! But it may be the most important thing you get out of this journal.

You know what's hard? Making friends as an adult. I saw a post on social media the other day that made me cackle. It said this:

How to make friends as an adult:

1. Say "we should hang!"
2. Do not hang.
3. Say "we should hang!" six months later.
4. Cancel.
5. Reschedule.
6. Respect their cancellation.
7. Reschedule.
8. Actually hang.
9. Say "we should do this more often!"
10. Die.[6]

I mean, is there anything closer to the truth? People say the dating scene is tough, and I wanna be like, "Yeah, but have you ever asked a new friend to hang out for the first time?"

But we have to, ladies! We have to seek out people who

are healthy, filled with joy, and who love the Lord. We can find these people at church, in small group, at book clubs, at the gym, or even online. The point is that we have to play an active role in creating and forming life-giving friendships—friendships we can lean into when we need great, godly women to check in with.

Hear

Perfume and incense bring joy to your heart.
And the sweetness of a friend comes from
their honest advice.
—PROVERBS 27:9

Respond

Make a list of all the things you would want in a friend you could check in with—someone you could be 100 percent honest and vulnerable with.

_____

_____

_____

_____

Now go back and look at your list. Time to be gut-level honest! Put a check mark beside all the qualities you listed that *you* exhibit in your everyday life.

Here's what I've learned—the best way to find a good friend is to be one. So be the friend you want to find. And then get to finding 'em!

Pray

Heavenly Father, help me to move beyond my comfort zone in search of new, check-in-worthy friends. Let me start with myself. The more I can show others love, the more love I will attract. I pray you put people in my path that I can reach out to, befriend, and check in with. I love you! Amen.

DAY 46

Read

Have you ever played the what-if game?

What if . . .

- I had gone to college instead?
- I had ended that relationship sooner?
- I had listened?
- I hadn't listened?
- I had said yes?
- I had said no?

Here's the thing about the what-if game: we're all losing. Okay? Nobody wins when you try to live in a moment that never was and never could be. But it's human nature to think back on big decisions and wonder a little bit. Like, *how would my life be different? How would I be different?*

Think

___

We've all been there. We made a decision and afterward thought, *Well, that wasn't the result I was hoping for. What if I had done things differently?*

I used to be the *worst* what-ifer. In recent years, after consistently checking in, I am improving. But around the time of my engagement ending, I what-ifed everything.

- *What if I'd waited longer to get engaged?*
- *Have I destroyed God's plan for my life?*
- *Is happiness now out of reach for me?*

I've got some good news for my fellow what-ifers. We serve a God who can redeem anything; he can restore anything, and he can heal anything. That's why he sent us Jesus—because he *knew* we'd be kinda dumb sometimes. That we'd sin. That we'd mess up.

He's a compassionate Father. He isn't going to doom you to a future of darkness just because you made a bad choice. He's always ready, arms open wide, for you to come back home.

Hear

[He] gave himself for us to redeem us from all wickedness and to purify for himself a people that are his very own, eager to do what is good.

—TITUS 2:14 NIV

Respond

What's one situation where you played the what-if game? Do a couple of them come to mind? Go ahead and list those too.

_____

_____

_____

_____

_____

What would it look like for you to receive redemption in the situation(s) you listed?

Remember, our idea of redemption doesn't always look like God's. He's more concerned with growing us and growing his kingdom than he is about tying a pretty bow at the end of every story. But you can be sure of this—he will do what's best for you.

Pray

Father, you are a loving God. You knew when you created us that we would need a savior. A savior to rescue us from evil. A savior to rescue us from ourselves. When I make a mistake, help me to acknowledge it, repent, and start over. Show me how pointless asking "What if?" is. Help me to be present in what you are doing in and around me. Amen.

DAY 47

Read

I got out of the hospital, we went back to filming, and I tried to pick up the broken pieces of my life and sort of tape them back together for the time being.

In the middle of that mess, I got the opportunity to get back on the Broadway stage in a Tony Award–winning revival of *Once on This Island*.

The new plan was: ignore my breakdown, make everyone happy, throw myself into a very work-heavy role, and hope for the best. Sounds solid, right? (It's okay. I'm rolling my eyes at myself too.)

So instead of checking in and asking myself tough questions, checking in with God and lining up my thoughts with his Word, checking in with my trusted friends, I shushed my common sense into silence and blindly forged ahead.

Think

You know what game I used to love? Hide-and-seek. Yo, no lie—I always found the best hiding places. I could cram my lanky arms and legs into any shelf, basket, or tiny closet. And then I could be reeeeal still. I was always the last person to be found.

But when it comes to life, being a good "hider" is not necessarily a good thing.

Wanna know one of the best hiding places? In plain sight. I filmed my reality show. I went to events. I signed on to a Broadway show. See, you never know what someone's hiding. You never know the pain or the suffering the smile on their face cost them.

What about you? Where's your favorite hiding place? Is it in your role as a mom? In your career? In your fight for social causes? In your relationships with men? In your ministry?

We all have some place we're at least tempted to hide when we're wounded, ashamed, or depressed. That's one reason why checking in is so important. It doesn't allow us to hide. In fact, it forces us to set our problems on the table one by one, surveying each under the light of truth.

Sooner or later, we've got to face ourselves. We've got to face God. And we've got to face the people who love us. And the longer you hide, the harder that's going to be.

Hear

Nothing God created is hidden from him. His eyes see everything. He will hold us responsible for everything we do.

—HEBREWS 4:13

Respond

When you don't want to deal with a conflict or struggle, where do you like to hide?

_____

_____

_____

_____

_____

What have been some of the consequences you've experienced as a result of hiding from your problems?

_____

_____

_____

_____

_____

The next time you feel like hiding from what's hard, what's one thing you can do or one person you can call to make sure you don't?

_____

_____

_____

_____

Pray

_____

Lord, you see everything. Everything we do, everything we think, and everything we feel. The next time I experience something difficult and feel like hiding, please help me to bring that situation to you. To open up to a friend. And to be honest with myself. Remind me to check in sooner rather than later, saving me and the ones I love from pain. Amen.

DAY 48

Read

The month of the show came, and with it, all the back-breaking bending.

I was in the middle of a phone conversation with Chad, and I don't even remember what we were arguing about. He made a comment that landed on me like a vat of hot lava.

Later I would learn that what I experienced next was a true psychotic break—worse in some ways than the episode in July that sent me to the hospital. All I know is, I blacked out and responded manically and ended things with him for good.

Looking back, do I blame depression for ending my engagement? Do I blame the imbalance of chemicals in my brain? Do I blame the Enemy? Do I blame myself?

The short answer is yes. All of those things played a role in the loss of my engagement.

However, we all have a personal responsibility to make choices that protect what we value. Since then, I have made every effort to guard my mental health at all costs.

Think

When we treasure something—whether or not it has a high monetary value—we protect it.

We invest in safes, safe-deposit boxes, fireproof filing cabinets, and protective coverings. We pay for identity protection coverage, alarm systems, insurance, and credit-report monitoring.

If it matters to us, we're making every effort to keep it safe and whole.

I wish we took this same approach to our mental health. I wish we prioritized our physical, emotional, and spiritual safety as much as we prioritize the safety of our possessions. See, guarding our hearts and minds is a job that only we can do. We can't hire it out or pass it off. Ultimately, it's completely up to us.

When I finally broke down, it would have been easy to start pointing fingers. Sure, the chemicals in my own body were working against me, but I *knew* what I needed to do. And I didn't do it. In the name of simplicity, I left my mind and my heart completely unguarded, vulnerable to all manner of evil.

And you know what? I have to own that. I have to step up and say that while I *was* very sick, I also chose to stay sick by not checking in.

Hear

Above all else, guard your heart,
for everything you do flows from it.

—PROVERBS 4:23 NIV

Respond

What are some things you own that you take precautions to protect or guard?

_____

_____

_____

_____

_____

How would you feel if your most prized possession on that list was severely damaged?

_____

_____

_____

_____

_____

Now, what precautions are you taking to guard your heart and mind?

_____

_____

_____

_____

What are three ways you can improve the protection of your mental health?

1. _____

2. _____

3. _____

If you treasure something, you will protect it. And I pray today that you install some sort of security system in your life that will sound the alarm when your mental health is compromised.

Father God, I have a responsibility to myself, to you, and to the people who love me to keep a close watch on my heart and mind. I pray your Holy Spirit will alert me anytime my mental health is at risk, and that I would quickly take action. Amen.

DAY 49

Read

The months that followed that December 2018 breakup (and breakdown) were bleak.

Have you ever broken a dish or poured out a bag of sugar on the floor by accident? Just really made a mess and wondered how you'd ever clean it all up or make it right? That's where I was. I was just like, *What have I done? What in this world have I done?*

Slowly, with time and prayer, the searing pain faded to a dull ache. I remember one day I got up and was sick of myself. Sick of being pitiful and sick of being sick. I looked in the mirror and said out loud, "It's time to get tough. You can and will do this."

Slowly, jagged piece by jagged piece, I walked around the wreckage of my life and started picking up the shards to see what could be salvaged.

Think

I saw a Twitter post the other day that I loved. It said, "A disco ball is hundreds of pieces of broken glass put together to become a magical ball of light. You aren't broken. You are a disco ball."[7]

Do you feel broken in some irreparable way? Has someone ever made you feel like damaged goods? Have you ever felt that something was wrong with you?

If you've ever felt alone in those feelings, let me give you a news flash—honey, you've got plenty of company.

But in my life there came a point when I had to get up, sift through the sharp pieces, and see what could be saved. The same is true for you. If you feel like you've experienced too much hurt and damage to ever be whole again, that's a lie straight from the Enemy's lips.

Sis, if no one has told you this, let me be the first—you ain't broken. And there is no situation that God can't repair. Maybe he'll do it in an unexpected way, but if we give him enough time, enough control, and enough obedience, he will make a disco ball out of shattered glass.

Hear

"But I will restore you to health
and heal your wounds,"
declares the LORD,
"because you are called an outcast."

—JEREMIAH 30:17 NIV

Respond

Think back to a time in your life when you felt broken—maybe even broken beyond repair. It could be right now. Describe how you felt (or feel). Make a list of emotions.

_____

_____

_____

Looking at those emotions, check in with God's words about you. Open your Bible or recall scripture. Line up what you're feeling against God's truth. What do you notice?

_____

_____

_____

_____

Just like a disco ball is made one broken piece of glass at a time, so healing comes in small doses. Little by little, day by day, God faithfully binds up our wounds and brings wholeness and restoration. As long as you do the work, before you know it, you'll be a magical ball of light!

Pray

God, I reject the lie that I'm damaged goods, because you say that through Christ, I am righteous, holy, pure, good, and whole. I pray that those words, those truths, would be what I remember when it's time to pick up the pieces of the messes I've made. And I pray that you would give me the courage to take those pieces, salvage what I can, and make something beautiful with my life. Amen.

DAY 50

Read

I've taken breaks from work from time to time, but never as intentionally as I did after my breakdown.

I took time for *me*. Time to press Pause on outward progress in order to press Play on inward progress. For the first time in twenty years, I wasn't concentrating on my music or my career.

Of course, I had heard the whisper of fear asking what pressing Pause would cost me. *Will I fade into irrelevance? Will I miss out on that comeback opportunity? Will I ever pick up the microphone again?*

But regardless of what it cost me to check in, I had come to realize it was a bargain compared to checking *out*, to being swallowed up by the depression that constantly lurked in the backdrop of my life.

Think

Want to know one word that I've grown to love? *No.*

The word *no* may be short, but it sure can pack a punch against mental illness.

See, what I needed most during the healing process was *rest.* Rest is different from sleep. Sleep happens in a measurable, definite way. Rest, on the other hand, is a little more abstract. You can rest physically, mentally, socially, and spiritually. Rest happens whenever we remove things, people, and commitments from our lives in order to focus on the things that are most important.

Rest feels unproductive, but in reality it's one of the best investments you can make in yourself and in your future. It's an opportunity to heal certain areas of your life that are currently overextended, burned out, or even broken.

But rest doesn't come to us on its own. Nope. We gotta "no" ourselves into rest periods. No to work. No to friends. No to the school PTO. No to the book club. Sometimes it means saying no to our own families.

During my season of rest, I could feel myself slowly waking up. Sometimes we have to check in with ourselves and take a step back. So I handed over my fears to God and did just that.

What kind of rest do you need in this season of your life? Don't be afraid of what you might lose. It pales in comparison to what you stand to gain through the power of rest.

Hear

The LORD replied, "I will go with you. And I will give you rest."
—EXODUS 33:14

Respond

Looking at the list below, circle three things you could take a rest from that would benefit you.

social media

going to the gym

work

church activities

dating

extended family

dieting

going to parties and events

volunteering

perfectionism

cooking

cleaning

carpooling

hosting

ministry

What would be at risk for you if you were to take an extended rest in those areas?

_____

_____

_____

_____

What's at stake for your mental and physical well-being if you *don't* take a rest in those areas?

_____

_____

_____

_____

Saying no for a season very well could give you the biggest yes in your future.

Pray

_____

God, saying no isn't easy. Especially when I'm saying no to people and things that I care about. But I also know that I need rest—extended rest. Because it's in these seasons that I can most clearly hear from you. Make me brave enough to disappoint others for the sake of my mental health—for the sake of having a better relationship with you. Amen.

DAY 51

Remember those labels we talked about earlier? Well, I went ahead and labeled myself as finished in the music industry.

Maybe this has happened to you.

Maybe, like me, one of life's heartbreaking disappointments ripped every meaningful label off your body so quick and mean that now you just feel raw. Maybe some of those labels were picked off in stages:

- Didn't get the promotion
- Another negative pregnancy test
- Parents sided with her again
- Uninvited to the party

Rip. Rip. Rip. Rip.

Or maybe those meaningful labels were snatched away from you all at once. And now you've labeled yourself as useless.

Think

We've talked about the labels given to us by others, but what about labels we've lost?

Maybe you were married and you wore the label of wife proudly. But then your husband changed his mind and ripped off that label when he left.

Maybe you were in ministry and gave all of yourself to the role. But then leadership changed, and that label was ripped from you without warning.

Maybe you were part of a group of friends and thought nothing could come between you. Only something did come between you, and loss of that label meant the loss of a piece of your heart.

The only thing worse than being labeled with something you *don't* want is having a label that you *do* want taken away.

It's in these moments that we have to check in with God the most. It's in these situations where we most need reminding of who we are. And that answer is not something that can be written on a removable label.

As children of the King, we are permanently branded as being enough. God loved us so much that he sent his Son, Jesus, to die for us. Jesus exchanged his righteousness for our rags. So now we have hope in heaven no matter what labels we wear while here on earth.

Hear

God so loved the world that he gave his one and only Son. Anyone who believes in him will not die but will have eternal life.

—JOHN 3:16

Respond

What are some labels you used to have but now don't?

_____

_____

_____

_____

_____

Which of those labels was the most painful to lose? Why?

_____

_____

_____

_____

_____

It's never going to feel good to lose a label you loved. But while things change here on earth, the things of heaven are eternal.

Which of the brandings (permanent labels) God has given you could replace the ones that were taken from you? Look back at day 5 for biblical examples of who God says you are.

_____

_____

_____

_____

_____

_____

_____

_____

_____

_____

Pray

_____

Lord, thank you that you never change. You are the same yesterday, today, and tomorrow. Help me to remember that you gave me the most important label—*yours*—and that it will never, ever be taken away from me. I love you. Amen.

DAY 52

Read

I think being busy is something we can all relate to. Everywhere I go, people look busy.

Don't you feel this? You look on Instagram and see someone's story. They've done prayed, worked out, enjoyed a breathtaking sunrise, juiced, made a gorgeous poached egg, cleaned out their closet, donated to charity, checked off their to-do lists, contoured their face, and met girlfriends for brunch, and you ain't even got the sleep crust out from the corner of your eyes yet.

You see that and you're automatically stressed out. *I should be doing more. I should be accomplishing more. I should at least pretend I've got it together.*

Think

I was in the drive-through at Hardee's getting a biscuit the other day, and there was a woman in the parking lot putting on mascara, eating, talking on the phone, and feeding her toddler. I wanted to step out of my car and salute this lady.

Here I am. Single. No kids. Some change in the bank. And I still find a way to feel overwhelmed with the demands of life. And if I sit too long thinking about that, I'll get depressed. I'll get anxious. My mind is off to the races!

If asking "What if?" is a game, comparing yourself to others is a trap.

But we all do this. And just like that, there's a dark cloud over our heads. We don't feel as positive, and we don't feel as happy, and we don't feel as good about ourselves.

We're caught in the comparison trap.

Hear

Each person should test their own actions. Then they can take pride in themselves. They won't be comparing themselves to someone else.

—GALATIANS 6:4

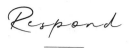

Respond

In what setting are you most tempted to get caught in the comparison trap? At church? Work? Out with friends? On social media?

_____

_____

_____

_____

Fill in the blank: Sometimes, I wish my life were more like _____.

What is it about that person's life that looks more attractive to you than your own?

_____

_____

_____

_____

One of the many problems with comparison is that there are always going to be people doing better than you in some way, and there are always going to be people who are not doing as well as you in some ways.

And neither set of those people have anything to do with who you are at your core.

If you were to compare your present self with your old self, what are three ways you've grown or improved?

1. _____

2. _____

3. _____

Pray

———

God, your Word tells me that it's better for me to measure my present self against my past self than it is for me to compare myself to other people. Convict my heart whenever I'm tempted to fall into the comparison trap. Help me to check in with these thoughts and dismiss them immediately, being grateful for all you have uniquely given me. Amen.

DAY 53

Read

One of Jesus' followers named Peter was giving advice to a church that was having some trouble. Here's what Peter said to the congregants: "Cast all your anxiety on him because he cares for you" (1 Peter 5:7 NIV).

We don't use the word *cast* this way a whole lot, but it just means to throw. Peter told them to cast their anxiety away. To throw it, to toss it.

My uncle used to take us fishing all the time. After putting your bait on the hook, you have to cast your fishing line into the water. Now, I've always been lanky, with long arms and long legs. And casting out a fishing line is not something a lanky preteen girl is going to nail the first time around. Or the second. Or the third. In other words, it took practice.

But this is exactly what Peter was saying: it takes practice. It takes practice to release the hold we have on our stress and anxiety.

Think

As a performing artist, I know firsthand how important practice is. When I was in Destiny's Child, we spent infinitely more time in rehearsals than we did onstage. Which I was thankful for because, out of the three of us, I consider myself the weakest dancer. So I'd keep trying, again and again and again, until I got the choreography.

I wish I'd been that determined to practice what Peter tells us to do. I wish I had cast my anxieties on God a whole lot sooner and a whole lot more often.

The Bible tells us to hurl our stress, our grief, our trauma, our disappointments, and our anxiety on him. Because when we do, these things will no longer be in our possession, but in his.

Hear

Cast all your anxiety on him because he cares for you.

—1 PETER 5:7 NIV

Respond

Grab a piece of paper. Make a list of all the things that are stressing you out right now. Anything that's giving you anxiety or making you feel depressed.

Now I want you to crumple up that paper and cast it away from you. That's right—I want you to throw it. Stand up and hurl that paper as hard you can. I can hear all my fellow OCD people right now, like, *And then just leave it there? A ball of paper? On the floor? Out in the open?*

Okay, here's the fun part. I want you to figure out a way to destroy the paper. You can burn it. You can tear it into shreds. Heck, you can squirt it with a water gun as an act of violence.

But as you're "casting your anxiety," remember: God gives us the option to do this with him on a spiritual level daily. Or a million times a day. However many times it takes for us to take our problems to his feet—and leave them there.

Pray

Heavenly Father, thank you for being a God who wants to bear my burdens. When I'm feeling overwhelmed, I pray you'd give a nudge—remind me that I have a choice. I can choose to deal with my problems on my own, or I can toss them to you and walk away lighter and full of peace. Amen.

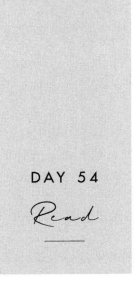

DAY 54

Read

My whole life I had my little list of what I thought a good daughter was, a good employee was, even what a good Christian was. Those lists ruled my life. If I crossed everything off, then I was okay. I was a good, acceptable person. If I didn't check all those boxes, then I was not a good person. I was actually a *bad* person. One of the many problems with this way of thinking is that it gives my lists power that only God should have. I'm serving these lists instead of serving God.

When Jesus died on the cross for me, he checked the only boxes that mattered:

- Redeemed
- Forgiven
- Whole
- Pure
- Blameless
- Good
- *His*

Now, instead of checking in with my own lists, I've learned to first check in with God's.

Think

Are you a list maker? I am. I'll get out my iPad every night and make a list of things I need to get done the next day in the Notes app. Lists are good. They keep us on track and on task.

But lists can be bad too. They can be harmful. They can even shame us, because they highlight all the things we haven't done that we've committed to. And if the sun sets on an unchecked task on one of my lists, I can't sleep. I'll toss and turn all night, wondering how I missed it.

We've all got lists floating around in our heads. To-do lists, sure. But other types of lists as well. Lists of what it means to be successful. Lists of what it means to be accepted by popular culture. Lists of what we think we need to be happy.

The problem with these lists is that they're rarely based on what God says—they're not his lists, they're ours. And when we try to check in with our lists *and* we check in with God's lists, it's like we're serving more than one master. Which, as the Bible points out, is impossible.

Hear

No one can serve two masters at the same time. You will hate one of them and love the other. Or you will be faithful to one and dislike the other.

—MATTHEW 6:24

Respond

Y'all already know what's coming!

I want you to make a list of what you think is required to be whole, healed, and happy. (Make sure your response reflects your actions and priorities!)

_____

_____

_____

_____

_____

_____

_____

_____

_____

Now open up that Bible or Bible app! Using Scripture as support, make a list of what God says is required to be whole, healed, and happy.

_____

_____

_____

_____

What's the biggest difference between the two lists?

_____

_____

_____

_____

Pray
___

Lord, it's impossible to be a servant to my lists *and* your lists. As a matter of fact, your lists seem pretty simple: Love God, love others. Use wisdom. Walk in truth. I pray that when I'm taking inventory of my life, I would check in with *your* lists first and finally. That I would find peace in knowing I'm checking off boxes to the tasks you've assigned and no one else. Amen.

Read

There's a difference between being transparent and being vulnerable. It's a very important difference that cost me plenty of relationships, even friendships, along the way. See, I have no issues with being transparent. Because with transparency, there's still a little bit of control. I can be transparent and say, "I'm going through some stuff right now. God is good! I'll be okay!"

But when you're vulnerable, you don't have that kind of control.

I'd say the biggest difference in being transparent and being vulnerable is that when you're vulnerable, no one has to ask you the tough questions because you are offering the truth freely. Transparency is simply offering information; vulnerability is revealing the thoughts behind your words and actions.

Vulnerability is going to cost you a little something every time because it's human nature to hide our weaknesses. It just becomes our habit.

Think

I don't think anyone suffering from anxiety or depression sits down at their desk and outlines a master plan to hide their suffering from their friends, families, and coworkers. I know I didn't. For many of us, it seems like everybody must already know how big of an emotional disaster we are.

During my lowest points, I was sure people were strategizing behind my back—coming up with ideas on how to stage an intervention to take me back to the hospital. Turns out, no one knew how critical my mental state had gotten because I wasn't being direct in my check-ins.

I was being transparent, but I wasn't being vulnerable.

Transparency says, "It's just been a bad day. I'll be okay—just need to get a good night's rest."

Vulnerability says, "I slept most of the day today because getting out of bed sounded like more than I was capable of. Yo, to be honest, I've been doing that a lot lately, and it scares me."

Listen, I know checking in this openly can be terrifying and almost intrusive. It's like walking down the middle of Times Square in your undies. But if all we're giving people when we check in with them is transparency, we might as well not be checking in at all.

Hear

Suppose we say that we share life with God but still walk in the darkness. Then we are lying. We are not living out the truth.

—1 JOHN 1:6

Respond

What's an example of something in your life that you're transparent about but not always vulnerable about?

_____

_____

_____

_____

_____

Why is it hard for you to be direct about your struggles in this area?

_____

_____

_____

_____

_____

What could happen if you continue to gloss over the depth of your insecurity, wound, or challenge?

_____

_____

_____

_____

_____

_____

_____

_____

_____

_____

Pray

―――――

Heavenly Father, I want to live out your truth. And that's going to require something of me—ruthless honesty and unfiltered vulnerability. Give me grace as I navigate this level of checking in. Because I know that on the other side of it is the wholeness and healing I've been longing for and which you've been longing to bring to me. Amen.

DAY 56

Read

Have you ever noticed that you can get stuck in a pattern of doing something so much that you don't even realize you're doing it?

For example, you find yourself saying the same things over and over in conversations. Stuff like "I mean" or "You know," or you say "umm" sixty times every time you're trying to tell someone a story. We do this to help us out when we aren't exactly sure what we're saying or to fill in pauses.

The problem is, very rarely do we feel like we have habits or behaviors we're stuck in. Instead of acknowledging our patterns, we make excuses for them.

Well, I had to have that extra glass of wine tonight because work was insane. Instead of, *I didn't come prepared for that meeting, and that's why I had a hard day at work.* It's just easier to prop up on that crutch than to check in with the truth that you aren't getting it done at the office lately.

Think

There are behavior patterns you have developed that are directly impacting your life that you've never viewed as habits. In fact, you've probably never thought about them at all.

These patterns are your default when you don't want to face the difficult parts of life. These patterns are your crutch. Maybe your crutch is partying. Going out. Drinking too much. You think, *We're just having fun. Nobody is getting hurt. It's not a big deal.*

Maybe your crutch is twisting the truth. You leave out details. You edit. You change the story enough to keep yourself out of trouble. *Oh, one little white lie won't hurt.*

Or your crutch is attention from men. Maybe you browse dating apps every night, visit certain sites, or hit up certain people who will tell you what you want to hear. You tell yourself it's not a big deal: *When I'm married, I'm not going to do this anymore.*

Maybe your crutch is overspending, overeating, not eating at all, gossiping, or zoning out online.

These crutches have become a way of life for you. They're patterns of behaviors. They're habits. And they're what's keeping you from being able to check in.

Hear

But here is what I tell you. On judgment day, everyone will have to account for every empty word they have spoken.

—MATTHEW 12:36

Respond

If you were to do a fearless inventory of the crutches in your life, what would you find?

_____

_____

_____

_____

What excuses or justifications do you give when you're leaning the weight of your anxiety and depression on these crutches?

_____

_____

_____

_____

Today's response involves another challenge that's going to push you a little bit. By now I hope you've identified at least one person you can vulnerably check in with. I want you to call, text, or email that person right now. Confess your crutches. Share what your justifications and your excuses sound like. Invite your friend to call you out when these habits reemerge in your life. *That* is checking in at its deepest, most life-changing level.

Pray

———

God, you are my rock and my fortress. You are the only source of strength that will never disappoint me. Surround me with people who will point to you when I'm defaulting to the things of this world that make me feel better in the moment but are pushing me toward spiritual bankruptcy over time. In you, I find something so much better than a crutch—I find healing. Healing that sets me on both feet, on solid ground. Amen.

DAY 57

Read

It's always been challenging for me to separate withholding forgiveness from protecting myself. But one thing I've learned is that you can cut someone out of your life and still forgive them. Being a forgiving person doesn't mean you have to be a dumb person too.

Here's how I see it. When we hold a grudge against someone, we replay the injury to ourselves like a movie reel. We feel like that person owes us something. Maybe it's an apology. But it's usually a lot more than that. And forgiveness simply takes that debt and cancels it out. *You don't owe me anything. The ledger is clear. I release you.*

I may not *feel* all warm and fuzzy for you. I may even decide that I just don't like you. But you don't owe me anything because I forgive you.

Think

If you're a follower of Jesus, you know how important it is to forgive others. We've already talked about it once in this journal, but what we didn't talk about was what comes *after* the forgiveness.

The answer to that may surprise you.

Sometimes, after forgiveness comes more forgiveness. When our wounds are especially deep, we may have to forgive someone more than once. More than twice. More than three times. Now, that doesn't mean we have to call them and verbally offer them forgiveness that many times. In fact, I'd advise against that.

Forgiveness is something accomplished inside of you—from your heart. And there are situations where resentment will show back up out of nowhere and you'll have to forgive someone all over again.

Forgiving someone doesn't mean you have to act like nothing happened. It doesn't make everything okay. Forgiveness cancels debt, but it doesn't erase what happened. There are natural consequences to people's actions. And it's okay to press Pause on a relationship until the sting of the injury has lessened. It's also okay to forgive someone and walk away. For good. God doesn't want us to be in relationships where we're constantly getting hurt.

Hear

Be kind and tender to one another. Forgive one another, just as God forgave you because of what Christ has done.

—EPHESIANS 4:32

Respond

You can find yourself in any of these three situations after you forgive someone:

1. Forgiving them again
2. Pausing the relationship
3. Ending the relationship

Which of these would be the most difficult for you to work through? Why?

_____

_____

_____

_____

_____

_____

_____

Think about the last person you had to forgive. Do you need to take any "after the forgiveness" steps? Have you truly canceled their debt in a way that's healthy and healed?

_____

_____

_____

_____

_____

_____

_____

_____

_____

_____

Pray

_____

God, Jesus' death wrote a check for all the debt my sin rang up on my tab. The forgiveness I get from you is complete and final. But I'm not you—I'm human. And I need the Holy Spirit's guidance when it comes to forgiving someone wholly and completely. Reveal what's required of me to show others love and grace while still guarding my mind and heart in the days that follow. Amen.

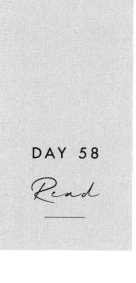

DAY 58

Read

Sometimes the hardest person to forgive is yourself.

After my engagement ended, I thought I'd never be able to look myself in the face again.

If I had been the only person hurt, it wouldn't have been so hard to forgive myself. But hurting the man I loved and the people I loved—the shame was deafening. It was all I could hear.

Think

If you're anything like me, the relationship you have with your-self has, at times, been borderline abusive.

I can be a straight-up jerk to me! If I were to treat others the way I've treated myself, I'd have no friends. Because there have been seasons in my life when all my depression and all my anxiety have convinced me that I am not worthy of love or respect—even from myself.

And when it comes to forgiving myself? To be honest, there are still some days when I wake up remembering things I've done, and by the time I've finished my coffee, I'm in a knock-down-drag-out with my own mind.

- *You are so stupid.*
- *Why did you do that?*
- *You knew better.*
- *You should have . . .*
- *You could have . . .*
- *If you'd just learn!*

Forgiving others can be so much easier than forgiving ourselves. *But both are equally important.* If we can't forgive ourselves, we'll get stuck. We'll stop progressing. We won't be whole or healed until we can offer grace and kindness to *everyone*, including the person staring back at us in the mirror.

Hear

Those who are kind benefit themselves.
But mean people bring ruin on themselves.
—**PROVERBS 11:17**

Respond

Get out a piece of paper and something to write with. Take a few minutes to write yourself a letter. That's right—a note from you to you. In the letter, I want you to name all the offenses you have against yourself. If you need help identifying those, think about any situation that still causes you to feel shame. Then, I want you to forgive yourself. Write those words down—*I forgive you.*

If you can, take the letter into a bathroom or something like that and read it out loud to yourself. Then, I want you to read it every day until the shame you're feeling is completely gone.

Pray

God, your Word talks a lot about forgiveness. It tells me that I should forgive everyone because you have forgiven me. Never does it say, "Forgive everyone . . . but torture yourself." No, you want me to be gentle with myself. You want me to have a good relationship with myself. You want me to live in freedom. And I can't do that if I'm constantly telling myself how worthless and without value I am. Today is the day I commit to showing myself the same grace I show others. Thank you for modeling complete forgiveness. I love you. Amen.

DAY 59

Read

Never in the history of the world has there ever been a more crucial time for us to be checking in.

When I first heard about COVID-19, I was in Los Angeles for award-show season. It was a really exciting time in my life because I was gearing up for a huge tour that would launch at the end of May and run through August. I was going to be onstage again, be an *artist* again. It felt like something *big* was about to start for me. Something *new*.

Fast-forward to March 2020. The world shut down. And with it, all my plans for the foreseeable future.

Think

In my lifetime, I've never experienced anything as shocking and life-altering as the COVID-19 pandemic that slammed the brakes on our entire culture.

I'd felt I was at the precipice of a career comeback. My breakdown and breakup were in the rearview mirror. I had done the hard work that checking in requires and, through God's miraculous grace, was on my way to peace, wholeness, and healing. For the first time in a long time, I felt excited about what my future held.

Then my future was canceled.

Just kidding—kinda. But you know what I mean. And my first thought was, *Oh no. This could be bad. What if I get depressed? What if I spiral?*

But you know what? I didn't. Sure, I was disappointed. Super bummed, y'all. But it's okay to be disappointed. What God doesn't want is for us to live in fear.

So I got ahead of any potential mental relapse by stepping up my check-ins. I took walks and searched my heart for signs of trouble. I scheduled FaceTimes. I talked to God more.

And you know what? I was okay. And I know that I'm going to be okay tomorrow. And the next day, and the next.

After all I've been through in my life, I have come to know as fact that God is in control, and as long as there's breath in these lungs, I will yield to his plans over my own every single time.

That's a kind of peace that I never thought was possible for me. It's a peace gained through a lot of work, a lot of humility, a lot of messing up and recalibrating, then trying again. It's a peace that only God can give—a peace received through checking in.

Hear

LORD, you will give perfect peace
to those who commit themselves to be faithful
to you.
That's because they trust in you.
—ISAIAH 26:3

Respond

Where were you when you first heard about the coronavirus (COVID-19)? What was your first reaction?

_____

_____

_____

_____

_____

_____

How have you handled the unknowns the pandemic has ushered into our everyday lives? In hindsight, would you have done anything differently?

_____

_____

_____

_____

Do you believe that God is in control? Do your actions and words support your response?

_____

_____

_____

_____

Pray

Father, 2020 is a year that I will never forget. The entire world changed in what felt like an instant, and it will never be the same. That can be a really scary thought. But I proclaim you as my King. I come into agreement with the truth that you are not surprised by anything—pandemics included. In every unfamiliar situation, help me to dig in and check in. That's the only way to maintain real joy, real peace. Amen.

DAY 60

Read

If it crosses your mind to reach out to someone to check in with them, don't hesitate. Don't check the scorecard to see who has texted or called more. Don't assume anything. Just do it.

You may have to move out of your comfort zone when it comes to checking in with others.

I've learned that I need to get off my recently called list, open up my contacts, and ask, *Who needs to hear from me right now?*

Think

I'm not a big phone talker. And I'm definitely not someone who often picks up the phone to call or text someone without a good reason. I don't like to bother people. And I don't particularly like to be bothered!

But if I've learned anything over the last few years, it's

this—we need one another. We do. We need others for wisdom, support, and community. We need to be cheerleaders for one another. Especially women!

Now that you know how to check in vulnerably and consistently, it's time for you to share what you've learned with someone—a friend, family member, coworker. Ask God to show you who.

We are never more like Jesus than when we're healthy enough to lift somebody up out of a pit. To give them hope. To give them love.

Hear

I give you a new command. Love one another. You must love one another, just as I have loved you.

—JOHN 13:34

Respond

Who can you check in with today to be a source of encouragement and love?

_____

_____

_____

_____

_____

_____

_____

_____

_____

_____

_____

_____

_____

Pick up that phone, sis. It's time for one last challenge. Send that text or make that call right now.

Pray

God, thank you. I can't say thank you enough for all the ways you've proven you love me fiercely and faithfully. I pray that I'd take what I've learned in this journal and apply it to my life in earnest. I pray for a lifestyle of checking in with you, myself, and others, growing in wholeness, healing, and faith, day after day. Amen.

NOTES

1. Robert Taibbi, "4 Key Ways Your Childhood Shapes You," *Psychology Today*, March 8, 2019, https://www.psychologytoday .com/us/blogfixing-families/201903/4-key-ways-your-childhood -shapes-you.
2. Hart Ramsey (@hartramsey), Twitter, January 23, 2020, 6:08 p.m., https://twitter.com/hartramsey/status/1220498469640720388.
3. Colleen Vanderlinden, "It's True—You Really Should Talk to Your Plants," The Spruce, updated March 9, 2021, https:// www.thespruce.com/should-you-talk-to-your-plants-3972298.
4. Daniel J. Powell and Wolff Scholtz, "Daily Life Stress and the Cortisol Awakening Response: Testing the Anticipation Hypothesis," *PloS One* 7, no. 12 (December 2012), https:// doi.org/10.1371/journal.pone.0052067.
5. Saul McLeod, "Defense Mechanisms," Simply Psychology, April 10, 2019, https://www.simplypsychology.org/defense -mechanisms.html.
6. Emily McKenna Winter (@EmilyMcWinter), Twitter, February 5, 2020, 11:13 a.m., https://twitter.com/EmilyMcWinter /status/1225090169239408640.
7. Judi Holler (@Judiholler), Twitter, February 5, 2021, 12:38 p.m., https://tweet.lambda.dance/JudiHoller/status /1357669940057227267.

ABOUT THE AUTHOR

$\mathcal{M}$ichelle Williams is a Grammy Award–winning recording artist and actress who rose to stardom as a member of the R&B mega group, Destiny's Child, and most recently appeared as the Butterfly on Fox's hit series *The Masked Singer*. Her successful solo albums include *Heart to Yours*; *Do You Know*; *Unexpected*, which spawned the internationally charted single, "We Break the Dawn"; and *Journey to Freedom*, which featured groupmates Beyoncé and Kelly Rowland on the single "Say Yes." Also a talented actress, she debuted on Broadway in *Aida* (2003) and starred in productions of *The Color Purple* (2007), *Chicago* (2009–2010), *What My Husband Doesn't Know* (2011), and *Fela!* (2013). Michelle is passionate about raising awareness about mental health and about sharing the lessons she has learned in her own struggle with depression.